ON MY WAY HOME

On My Way Home

Pat + John

Joy for the Journey

Ingrid Trobisch Youngdale
and
Katrine Stewart

Ingrid Trobisch Youngdale

Quiet Waters Publications
Bolivar, Missouri
2002

For information contact:
>   Quiet Waters Publications
>   P.O. Box 34, Bolivar MO 65613-0034.
>   E-mail: QWP@usa.net.
For prices and order information visit:
>   http://www.quietwaterspub.com

Cover design: Myron Sahlberg
Cover photo: Maja Sahlberg
Tree drawings: Ingrid Trobisch Youngdale

ISBN 1-931475-11-3
Library of Congress Control Number: 2002090643

For two of the best, Walter and Lauren,

and my six sons and six daughters

CONTENTS

Mount Kilimanjaro

ONE

OLD MOSHI
BLESSED IS THE DAWN

"To live is to be slowly born."
~Antoine de St. Exupery~

Mt. Kilimanjaro towers over the East African highlands of Tanzania. No wonder the Africans like to call this mighty mountain The Throne of God or The Shining Mountain. Like a taciturn giant, it stands as an ever-present witness to all that lives and moves in its domain. I was born on the slopes of this mountain in the small settlement named Kidea, formerly known as Old Moshi. My parents insisted it was one of the most beautiful spots on the face of the earth.

Word spread quickly of my arrival at that early morning hour of February 17, 1926. Even before dawn a chorus of rejoicing women of the local Chagga people came to sing for my mother, welcoming me into their midst. Their melodious, rhythmic chanting surrounded the mission house and filled it with a special air of joy.

Awakened by the unusual sounds, my four-year-old brother Paul tottered out of the boys' room, rubbing his eyes in wonder.

"But it's only a little bit morning," he told his father.

"You're right, son, your new little sister didn't even wait till the new day arrived. Have a look at who I'm holding in my arms." Carefully he stooped down to Paul's level and let him peer at the sleeping baby wrapped in a warm blanket. The entire bundle fit perfectly into the crook of his father's strong arm.

"Your life won't ever be the same again with a sister around! Let's not wake your little brother John yet, but you and I can go to the veranda and show the baby to our visitors."

Proudly, father and son walked out into the African dawn. The chanting women danced with joy. As the sun slowly rose into view, The Shining Mountain made its majestic appearance through the morning clouds.

I am convinced that at this moment the close bond that I have shared with my father over a lifetime was formed. In my mind I see him holding me up and saying, "Look, my daughter, at this wonder-filled world you have entered. It is amazing and it is yours for the taking. Go for it!"

Five days later I was baptized at the Old Moshi chapel. My parents and their friends, Pastor and Mrs. John Steimer, placed me symbolically in the safe arms of Christ. Pastor Steimer pronounced, with a loving twinkle in his eyes, the baptismal promise he had chosen: "God will command His angels to protect you wherever you go" (Psalm 91:11). He gave us a small angel picture with text in Swedish illustrating this verse which has accompanied me on my way home. I am afraid I have kept those angels frightfully busy.

If I am asked about the validity of infant baptism, I can only reply the same way my eight-year-old niece did when asked this question, "All I know is that my parents put me in the arms of Jesus, and he hasn't dropped me yet."

I was named Ingrid after my father's grandmother and Johanna after my father's mother. All of my grandparents have come from Sweden. Ingrid comes from the Scandinavian and means *daughter of the king* or *hero's daughter*. Johanna, which is the feminine form of John, means *God is gracious*. My family name, Hult, is the same as the English word, *holt*, which means *a safe place, a wood*. English authors speak of a *rabbit's holt*. Astrid Lindgren's mother, the popular Swedish children's author, also had the maiden name and came from the same region as my grandfather Hult.

I realize now that the names that were so lovingly chosen for me at birth have become life-long callings. They have challenged me in unexpected ways. To be the daughter of a king and a hero has not just made me feel special, but has also meant long stretches of loneliness in my life, of missing my peers, and of not daring to admit fear. Without the amazing gift of God's grace, many times I would not have had the strength to go on. As my family and the readers of my books can attest, my search for a safe place in this world has become a lifelong quest.

"The beginning is half of the whole."
~Plato~

My mother said I was a good traveler. I was just three weeks old when on March 7, 1926, we embarked on a ship in the port city of Mombasa which would take us through the Red Sea, the Suez Canal, the Mediterranean, and up the Atlantic coast to Bremerhaven, Germany. It was time for my parents to go home on leave. My father had already been in Africa for more than seven years, and my mother for five.

Why should I not be a good traveler when my mother and father were always close by and I had my safe place? My mother had carefully lined a rectangular wicker basket and placed a firm kapok mattress in it. This was not only my place those first months of life, but was also the first bed for my younger siblings. It had a place of honor on the dresser in my parent's room. When it was no longer needed for the baby of the family, it served as a laundry basket for the fresh sheets dried on the clothesline on our Ozarkian homestead.

I was not my parents' first-born daughter. The little grave of baby Ruth Eleanor lies on another slope of the Shining Mountain at Machame station where my parents served when they first came to Tanzania. As a family we celebrated Ruth's birth and death on July 11. It was the only time I recall, as a child, seeing tears in my mother's eyes. She looked at the little green vase filled with fresh flowers on the kitchen cabinet and told me that this vase had been given to her at Ruth's funeral. I used to hold the vase in my hands, this symbol of my sister, and try to imagine how she would have looked and what it would have been like to have an older sister. But hearing about her also made heaven more real. I knew that when the time came, she would be there ready to welcome her parents and siblings.

"Begin to weave and God will give the thread."
~German Proverb~

It seems fitting to weave a story of the birth and life of another little girl into my life's tapestry here. In 1998, I visited Sweden as the guest of Annette Fogelquist. Her father, John Steimer, had baptized me. Annette, who had spent happy years on the mission station close to ours on the slopes of Kilimanjaro, was as dear to me as an elder sister. Life can have a strange way of filling the deep yearnings of our heart when we least expect it to happen. As we sat together in her cozy red summer cabin, Annette told me this story:

My husband and I were sent to South Africa by the Swedish Missionary Society. We were very happy there and God gave us five children. My husband's work as a builder was sorely needed. However, when we came home on furlough for a well-deserved rest, he was

*killed by a careless motorcyclist. My husband was standing in front
of the church hall where he was to give a lecture when the motorcyclist,
speeding and not able to make the curve, caught my husband's coat
in his handlebars and dragged him to his death.*

Annette, in her early thirties, and with five small children,
studied church music, practicing early in the morning while
her children were sleeping. As a single parent she became an
organist and choir director and also a hostess for missionaries
on furlough. She reminded me of Katherine Hepburn—the
way she dressed and wore her hair. She sparkled with energy
and joy.

Her oldest son, Sven, became a pastor, and with his wife
accepted a call to Tanzania to be missionaries. While there,
they made a trip to the Kilimanjaro area where his grandparents had been pioneer missionaries together with my parents.
Sven wanted to find the grave of his mother's little sister who
had also been called Ruth, just like my sister. Annette showed
me a picture of her sister, a beautiful little girl of three who
one day had become very ill. After a few hours of suffering,
Ruth had died and had been buried close to the chapel her
father had built. Annette continued her story:

*Sven saw an ancient-looking woman seated on the steps of the chapel
and spoke to her in Swahili. 'Can you show me the cemetery and
take me to the grave of baby Ruth Steimer?' he asked without much
hope that the woman could help him.*

*Her wrinkled face lit up in disbelief when he told her who he was.
'Come with me,' she said and unhesitatingly led him to the spot
where a worn wooden cross was still standing with the name of Ruth
Steimer. 'I know,' she said, 'because I was the Ayah (nursemaid) for
little Ruth. When your grandparents came and told us the story of
Jesus, I didn't know what to think. But when I saw the white man
and his wife weeping just like we weep when we lose a child, I knew
they were real. That is when I listened and became a believer.'*

For sixty years the Ayah had faithfully tended the little grave.
Annette showed me a part of the cross that Sven had brought
home to her. He had carved her sister's name and the dates

of her birth and death on it. We wept together, and then I reminded her that today there is a healthy, strong church in Tanzania where our parents pioneered and laid their precious daughters to rest. In fact, with 2,300,000 members, this is the largest Lutheran Church in Africa.

"The world is round and the place which may seem like the end may also be only the beginning."
~*Ivy Baker Priest*~

As a child, I relived my birth many times in my dreams. Even as an adolescent I often had the same dream with a glorious sense of freedom and light at the end. I dreamt I was in a very small place that I had entered through the keyhole in my father's desk in my parents' bedroom. Somehow I struggled free, but then I was falling, falling. I heard and felt the rushing of a waterfall. I saw this waterfall gushing forth into a canyon, and I had an indescribable feeling of joy. I was free, and at the same time I was sheltered. It's no wonder I was drawn to prenatal and perinatal psychology in later years and enjoyed a lively dialogue with obstetricians and childbirth educators worldwide. Whether acknowledged or not, our birth stories form a deep, primordial imprint on our lives.

Twice I was able to visit my birthplace. The first time my mother was with me, so she could show me the very room where I was born in the Bruno Gutmann Home. Bruno Gutmann was a pioneer German missionary who came to Chaggaland in 1902. He was able to record the history and customs of the Chagga people as no other. In his missionary activity Gutmann came into contact with the three primal ties of clan, neighborhood, and age. He felt strongly that these were the points of contact for evangelization as well as developing and establishing Christian congregations. This was the way to reach the whole family and the whole clan with the gospel, rather than just individuals.[1]

That visit was in 1961, and the sturdy building was being used as a birth clinic for Chagga women. It was another 35 years before I could return with two of my sons and show them. The birth clinic was still there. The nurse-midwife took us through and showed us the delivery room. I congratulated the African mother who had just given birth in the same room where my mother had given birth seventy years earlier.

"The family is the best landing place for the gospel," both my father and my husband fervently believed. In fact, this was their passion and the joy of their ministry.

"What is your passion?" I often ask my family and friends. I've found that *passion* and *compassion* are related. Africa, the land of my birth, the place where my father is buried and where four of my children were born, is the continent of both my passion and my compassion. That is why I cannot tell my story without relating it to this land and people that I love. I suffer when I sense a certain lack of curiosity on the part of even fellow Christians to hear the story of what has happened and is happening in this great continent.

The promise and the blessing of my birth morning have left a gilded imprint on every new morning in my life. I close this chapter with the words I have used and sung since childhood as I greet the new day and thank God for the miracle of new beginnings:

The steadfast love of the Lord never ceases,
His mercies never come to an end;
They are new every morning,
Great is thy faithfulness.
Lamentations 3:22-23

The Hult Family

T W O

Roots • A Safe Place

"The past is the place we view the present from."
~Frederick Buechner~

I spent the first year of my life making two ocean voyages and traveling across three continents. In hindsight I begin to understand my lifelong desire for a *safe place*.

Hard maple trees lined our driveway in the rolling hills of the southern Missouri Ozarks. The limbs of my favorite tree had arranged themselves so perfectly that even a small child could find refuge in them and lean against the sturdy trunk without fear of falling. Sometimes, especially when my father was away, I climbed into that tree to my safe place where no one could see me. I hugged the trunk as if it were my only friend, and I let my tears flow. It felt so good to hold on to something that is constant and could always be found when I needed it most. At other times I felt a surge of power as I sat in the branches and could let the world go by. Looking at things from above changed my perspective and made my own little worries become smaller by the minute.

After leaving the slopes of The Shining Mountain with their three young children, my parents visited Germany and Sweden on their way home to America. Their first stop was in Leipzig, Germany. Little did I realize what a prominent role that city would play in my future. Soren Kierkegaard once said that life must be lived forward, but can only be understood backward. Submitting myself to the hard discipline of writing an autobiography has helped me to comprehend his words. I begin to *understand my life backward* in a new way. It is like climbing into that childhood tree and looking down on my life with a perspective that has moved beyond time. I see my life and what I made of it the way God might see it, and I am simply awed by the way He has cared for me.

My father, Ralph Hult, had been serving as Superintendent of the American Lutheran Mission in Tanganyika. He wanted to confer with Leipzig Mission Director Ihmels about the future cooperation of American and German missionaries in that country. Tanganyika was no longer a German colony, but a part of British East Africa. Later, upon independence in 1962, its official name would be Tanzania, a combination of Tanganyika and Zanzibar. Their talks resulted in a new harmony and understanding, assuring the Germans they could continue to build on the fine work they had started. The American missionaries then would concentrate their pioneering efforts on the central plains of Tanzania.

Just a few blocks from where my father met with the German mission authorities in Leipzig, his future son-in-law was growing up. Walter, then a happy three-year-old, was being carefully nurtured as the first-born son of his teacher parents. How I was to meet Walter is just one of the many surprises God had planned for my life. Ralph and Walter were never to meet on this earth.

After leaving Germany, my parents enjoyed quiet and restful months in Sweden. They were refreshed in body and soul while staying at a retreat house for missionaries in Malmo. There they found a safe haven that gave them a vision for a future ministry. If they could not return to Africa because of economics or church politics, perhaps they could create such a place of peaceful shelter in their own country where Christian workers could come for rest and healing.

As a symbol of that dream my mother purchased a beautiful piece of Swedish woven cloth to be used as a table cover. She never had time to embroider it, so she gave it to me two decades later with the words, "Please make something beautiful from this."

As a wedding gift, a Danish colleague embroidered a Scandinavian design on it. This prized tablecloth has graced all the homes that I have had—in Africa, Austria, and now the Ozarks—reminding me of my Swedish heritage. Only very few material possessions have remained constant in my turbulent life of geographical moves. This piece of cloth is one of them, a symbol of a *safe place*—no matter where in the world I have found myself.

"Going home is a lifelong journey."
~Henri Nouwen~

Everything worth remembering is simple and true and real. We spent the remainder of our year of home leave in Wahoo, Nebraska, where my father rented a house next to my beloved grandmother's home. Johanna Mathilda Lind Hult had been born in Härlunda (near Skara), Västergottland. She left Sweden with her parents and three siblings to come to the United States in 1872. My earliest memories of a *safe place* consisted of the sheltering space under my grandmother's freestanding kitchen range. There I could play quietly to my heart's content, safe from my two big brothers.

My sister Veda was born when I was 18 months old. As an adult I once shared with her that I could not remember ever sitting on my mother's lap.

"Of course you couldn't," she said. "I came along and pushed you off."

I've pondered why this question only came up between us as adults. I don't recall ever feeling jealous towards my siblings. I was fiercely proud of each one. As a child I had certainly not felt neglected. Perhaps it was because I knew I could always crawl up on my father's lap. There was a special affinity between the two of us. As his oldest living daughter after two sons, I cashed in on his love whenever I could.

Then came the Great Depression of the 1930s. It took our mission board three years to conclude that they could not do mission work in both West and East Africa. Eventually they decided to concentrate their forces in East Africa. It was more feasible economically for an American mission to work in an English-speaking territory like Tanzania, East Africa, than in French-speaking West Africa. My father was in a quandary. After his earlier pioneer travels in West Africa, he had promised specifically the Sara people in Chad that he would return to them. While waiting for guidance, he pastored a Swedish Lutheran church in Verona, a small town in southwestern Missouri.

It wasn't long before my parents decided that the Ozark region was a good place to raise their growing family. In 1931 they purchased a 40-acre fruit farm just outside of Springfield. We named it Bethany Homestead, because it was to be like the home in Bethany where Jesus loved to stay. It did become our safe place for the next decade. At that time I was four—the age when a child begins to put down roots which will last for life.

When relatives visited, often coming from the rich farmlands of Nebraska and Illinois, they would dubiously examine the rocky soil of our land. "Ralph, what in the world grows here?" they asked my father.

"Trees and children," was his quiet answer.

Father's friend and colleague, Ludwig Melander—Uncle Lud as we called him—asked yet another question, "Ralph, are you sorry that you're not serving on the mission field?"

"But I do have my mission field," Father insisted. "It's right here. My children are my mission field."

The walls of our small house were made out of those very rocks that our relatives were questioning. Above the reed organ in the living room, Daddy hung a painting of the *SS Gripsholm*, the famous Swedish ship that had taken our family across the Atlantic in 1926. It provided a window to the world in our three-room stone cottage, as did the six by eight-foot library map of Africa which Daddy mounted on another wall. The third painting he chose hung in a prominent place by the front door. It showed St. Ansgar preaching and holding up a cross to some wild-looking men.

"St. Ansgar was a remarkable man who left his home in France in the 9th century and became the first missionary to Scandinavia," he explained to us.

No wonder the Hult children grew up with a special place in their heart for world missions.

Our little home seemed blessed in many ways. Love abounded despite material hardships. The growing family—eventually we were five girls and five boys—soon could not fit under one roof. We had two little cabins to sleep in—one for the older boys and one for the older girls. I have heard that sibling relationships influence us even more that our relationship with our parents. In the end, a sibling relationship is the only one that lasts throughout life. Some researchers believe that it is almost impossible psychologically to disassociate oneself from a sibling as one might from a friend or spouse. That is why cutting this unique bond is so painful.

As I look back on my life, I can see how important being close to my siblings has been for me. Our interaction and interdependence became even deeper after we lost our father so early and unexpectedly.

Trees were the joy of my childhood. They beckoned me quietly outside, promising shelter and beauty and time to dream. Inwardly I struggled to balance my need for solitude with the countless demands of family life and helping my mother.

How I loved to play in the woods with my brothers and sisters! I remember even going out during gentle, refreshing rains and watching the green leaves wash into browns and then back again as the seasons changed. I listened to the thousand sounds of imaginary dripping fountains, becoming keenly aware of a fresh new spirit in the air and in my heart. My brothers explored every inch of the woods surrounding our home and climbed trees as far up as they could go, safely or not so safely. They would swing on precariously dangling vines or see how high they could build a pile of wood before it toppled over. I loved to make a house plan on the ground, using sticks to lay out the rooms. It was my way of creating new inner spaces when I felt crowded by chores and the many expectations the adult world seemed to have of me.

Three times a day we gathered for meals around the large rectangular table which had once been used to display merchandise in a general store. As we sat down to our bowls of hot cereal with the morning sun streaming through the French windows, we joined hands and sang:

Again Thy glorious sun doth rise,
I praise Thee, O my Lord,
With courage, strength and hope renewed,
I touch the joyful chord.

Mother cooked good food and was able to feed her ten children on a small budget.

"You have a wonderful mother, Ingrid," one of my aunts said to me. I looked at my mother with new respect after that, for I thought all mothers did what my mother did. Now I know what an unusual woman she was.

In the evening, after a healthy supper that always included fruit and vegetables from our own garden, Daddy read to us from Hurlburt's Bible Storybook. Standing around the little reed organ which we all learned to play, we would sing our favorite hymn *Children of the Heavenly Father.* Then we prayed in unison Psalm 67:1 and 2. These verses are a request for God's blessing that *His way might be made known upon the earth,*

His salvation among all nations, and they were engraved in my parents' wedding rings.

While pointing out places and travel routes on the wall-sized map of Africa, Daddy would often tell us of his adventures as a pioneer missionary when he traveled for eighteen months in the interior of West Africa. Leaving his new bride in the United States, he went to West Africa, visiting more than one hundred tribes in northern Cameroun, Chad, and French Equatorial Africa.

I never questioned his reasons for leaving my mother behind, nor did I fully understand until later the sacrifice this must have meant for both of them. I was fascinated by the elaborate leather-bound copy of the Koran that he had received as a gift from the great Chief Rey Bouba in northern Cameroun. Another chief, this time of the Sara tribe in Chad, had welcomed my father with the words:

"For five years we have looked up and down the road waiting for a man of God to come and teach us. We have heard the name of Allah, but we don't know how to speak to him. Please stay with us."

And so my father had promised them he would be back. It took a generation for that to happen—through his own children.

"Life is the first gift, love is the second,
and understanding the third."
~Marge Piercy~

A favorite author, Willa Cather, once said that where we spend the years between four and fourteen—providing they are happy and without undue trauma—will be the place where our roots are formed. In my case this was certainly true. Regardless in which continent I happened to be living, I always measured distance by how far it was from Springfield,

Missouri. That was and is the center of the world for me. Now in my later years, I realize that I can only do the traveling I do because I know where my roots are, and I have a place where I am at home. And because I have a place, I can also be a place for others.

When I was five and a half years old, my parents deemed me ready to go to the one-room rural school adjacent to our property where Paul and John, my two older brothers, attended. There were thirty pupils in eight grades—all in one room. I don't remember being taught how to read. I had already figured it out from the children's books we had at home which my brothers read to me. We had a good library at school too. It was pure joy for me to read and read in the sheltered atmosphere of the schoolroom as I tuned out the hum of the other children reciting their lessons. I was even sad if our teacher announced that there would be no classes for two days because she would be going to a Teachers' Convention. The experience of attending a one-room rural school stood me in good stead when I later taught the children of missionaries in a similar setting in Africa.

Sitting on the hard school bench from 9:00 a.m. until 4:00 p.m. with an hour break for lunch was serious business. I now had a new authority in life: my beloved teacher Flo Young. She seemed like the most beautiful woman in the world to me with her deep blue eyes, porcelain skin, and wavy black hair. I wasn't the only one who thought so. Years later she told me the story of one of my classmates in first-grade, Jim Miller, who was smitten by her charms. She happened to be boarding with his parents that year, as was the custom in rural communities.

Besides teaching us, she was also responsible for cleaning the schoolhouse. One day, after she finished her janitorial duties, she picked up her books and was ready to walk the mile home with her young admirer. About half way there, he couldn't keep quiet any longer. "Miss Flo," he said, "I sure do need a kiss."

She smiled as she put down her books on the pathway and gave him a warm hug and a kiss.

Birthdays were special. Since mine was in February, it was usually cold. One year, before the big girls had to move their sleeping quarters to the cottage, I woke to the sound of my father making a fire in the little iron stove in the living room. I kept my eyes shut and pretended to be asleep as my big brother Paul reminded Daddy: "Today is Ingrid's birthday. I will never forget when she was born. There were a lot of African women singing outside our house, and they woke me up. At first I was scared. Then you came and showed me the new baby in your arms."

"The sounds and the excitement of that morning will stay with me forever," my father replied in a hushed voice, trying not to wake anyone still sleeping or even just pretending to be asleep. "Ingrid's birth filled my heart with great joy. I knew like I never did before that we were where God wanted us to be." Their words made me feel special.

"Joy is the simplest form of gratitude."
~Karl Barth~

At the breakfast table my family sang happy birthday to me, and I was always a little embarrassed because I didn't know what to do—sing with them or try not to show my pleasure. In the evening we always celebrated the same way. Mother put a special white hand-woven African cloth on our table instead of the usual oilcloth. She lovingly placed two ebony candlesticks in the middle. My parents' prized wedding gift, a cut-glass crystal bowl made up the centerpiece. It was filled with a special pudding or fruit dessert. A round two-layered birthday cake decorated with the right number of candles crowned the crystal bowl. We all held hands and sang together at this festive time. I knew I belonged and never need fear being abandoned or emotionally unattached.

I recall little friction between my parents in those years. When they needed to discuss a difficult issue, Daddy would ask Mother to go for a walk with him. She handed me the gravy stirrer with instructions for finishing the meal, and off they would go. She listened to my father's dreams and was his steadfast encourager during a very discouraging time. I remember one particular time when he shared his dreams at the dinner table in a rather bitter tone.

"Ralph, aren't you being cynical?" Mother said quietly. Since this word was not in my ten-year-old vocabulary, I looked it up in our family dictionary. Was my father really being sarcastic, even scornful?

Years later, my lawyer, Jack Appelquist, who had known my parents in his youth, said to me, "It always impressed me to see how your parents bore their suffering with dignity and a lack of bitterness during the depression, when they had to live on a very inadequate income." Perhaps it was a lesson they had learned from their African friends who know how to quietly accept suffering—without bitterness or complaint.

"Do not worry about anything, but in everything by prayer and supplication with thanksgiving let your requests be made known to God."
~Philippians 4:6~

We had purchased our 40-acre farm on a plan financed by the Home Owners' Loan Corporation. Our monthly HOLC payment was $17.25. Every time we sold a bushel of apples from our fruit trees, we put the money in a silver cup with my father's initials on it. The good apples picked from the trees sold for a dollar a bushel. The ones picked up from under the trees sold for 25 cents a bushel. I recall the last day of July 1933, in particular. We all watched as Daddy emptied out his silver baby cup to see if we could pay the HOLC. Together we counted its contents. Exactly enough to pay our mortgage for that month! This was one of my first real lessons in faith.

Another incident I remember vividly is when Daddy came home from town one day with his face alight. He proudly showed Mother a ten-dollar bill which a friend had given him for his large family.

"Wonderful! Now we can get linoleum for the kitchen floor," was Mother's first joyous response. "It will be so much easier to clean."

"Oh, I've already looked at second-hand radios. We can get a nice one for ten dollars," Daddy replied with a broad grin.

We got the radio. This elevated my father to hero status in my eyes. In retrospect only have I begun to understand the level of sacrifice required of my mother as she tried hard to be his soul mate and encourager even if it meant going without linoleum in the kitchen.

Sitting together in the evening and listening to special programs on our precious first radio soon became a family tradition. When the Bell Sunday Evening Hour came on, Daddy would turn off the lights and as we sat in a close family circle, he would explain the music to us. We listened. This manner of appreciating music became a habit and accompanied us all into our adult lives.

My father was patient, long-suffering, stubborn, and sentimental. He never shamed us, his children. He believed in us. And most important of all, I knew that he loved my mother and she loved him. They were a living witness to what Joseph Bayley expressed in his poem *A Psalm of Love*:

> *Thank you for children*
> *brought into being*
> *because we loved.*

God of love,
keep us loving
so that they
may grow up whole
in love's overflow.

After the Sunday morning worship service at home, Daddy taught each one of us older children our Sunday School lessons individually. We sat with him at his desk with our Bible Storybook in front of us. I recall one Sunday just before Christmas when he told me about Gabriel, the angel who came to Mary and told her she would have a baby even though she was a virgin and had not slept with a man. It was the perfect moment for Daddy to tell his nine-year-old daughter where babies came from—the miracle of life. He also told me that intercourse between a man and woman belongs only in marriage.

"Did you sleep with Mother before you got married?" I asked him in confidence.

He assured me that he had not, and he went on to say, "Ingrid, I want you to think about the future," he told me in his kind voice. "Although you're not even ten yet, it's not too early to begin praying for the one who will one day be your husband." I looked into his eyes and took his advice seriously. From that day on I trustingly prayed for my future life partner.

If my father taught me the lessons of faith, it was my mother who taught me the essentials of childcare. A new baby in the family was a source of great joy. We older children ran to school to see who would be the first to tell the good news to our teacher and our close neighbors. We listened proudly to the announcer of our local radio station telling of the new arrival in the Hult family.

Since I was the oldest daughter, I had the privilege of bathing the baby after Mother had shown me how to do it. She spread out a large bath towel on the dining room table—the same table that we used for our family meals. Then she took a white enameled dishpan, filled it with warm water which she had heated on the kitchen stove, carefully testing the temperature with her elbow and inviting me to do the same. First she tenderly cleaned the baby's face with a soft washcloth. She made her own cotton swab and dipped it in the precious bottle of olive oil which had been purchased for the new baby. She skillfully cleaned the nostrils and the ears. After soaping the baby's scalp, she rinsed it while holding the baby on her left arm over the bathtub, carefully supporting the head.

Always in eye contact, talking to the baby, she soaped the little body. I watched in amazement as she expertly lifted the baby to the water, immersing the body while firmly holding up the baby's head. What joy as the baby relaxed in the water, splashed, and made happy gurgling noises. When the bath was finished, a cry of protest was usually forthcoming. Now she patted the skin dry and massaged the little wriggling body with a few drops of olive oil. I got to choose the clothes for the day and helped dress the baby—the little cotton shirt with tabs on the side where the cloth diaper would be pinned on and then a romper or a little dress. Mother showed me how to lay out the flannel receiving blanket like a baseball diamond, first folding up a flap to cover the baby's legs and then wrapping the two sides firmly around the body with just enough blanket at the top to keep her head warm.

Now it was Mother's turn to take a rest while she breast-fed the baby, and I cleared the table and put away the baby things. Could Mother have known, as she faithfully nurtured life, that four of her daughters would become nurses, working in busy delivery rooms, hospital wards, and on lonely mission stations, and that her son John would be a beloved pediatrician? When my first child, Katrine, was born in the high plains of northern Cameroun, I was at ease in caring for her because of what my mother had taught me. It is no small tribute to Mother that her ten children should all live into their seventh and eighth decades.

A *safe place* need not always be a physical space. Among other things it can also be a garment. As an adult, one of my sisters served as a missionary nurse in Tanzania. She was single and felt lonely and out of place when she came on home leave. One day she went shopping for a new winter coat, something she needed for the cold Minnesota weather. She found just the right one waiting for her on the rack. It seemed to have her name on it. When she slipped it on, it immediately became more than a garment just to keep her warm. It turned into a symbol of shelter for her against the storms of life. All winter she wore it, and her heart was strangely comforted. People complimented her on how well the coat highlighted her fair skin and copper-colored hair.

The day came when she had to return to her assignment in Africa. She would not need her coat there, so she gave it to a friend. Little did she realize how much her heart would bleed. She felt like she had given away a part of herself.

Years later our little Bethany cottage had to be torn down because it was no longer up to the standards of other homes in the area. My sister Eunice and brother John watched as the bulldozer pushed over the rock walls of their childhood home. They wept. Mother, who had given birth to five of her children there, looked on dry-eyed.

"Come, let's move on," she said. And then she added, "It was always a cold house in winter."

Strangely, none of us children knew that it was cold. She had kept us warm. She had kept us safe.

Ingrid and her grandmother awaiting news of the Zamzam

THREE

A ROOM OF MY OWN

"Whether we like it or not,
asking is the rule of the Kingdom"
~C. H. Spurgeon~

Joy of joys! Only slowly did I dare open my eyes. Had I just dreamed of Grandmother's voice calling me to come to breakfast? The clean white sheets felt like heaven. I luxuriously stretched and curled my toes while taking in my new surroundings. The mattress seemed like the most comfortable one I had ever slept on, firm and yet molding itself to my body, the body of a lanky thirteen-year-old. I weighed less than a 100 pounds, but had shot up to a height of five foot seven.

Everything was in order in the tidy little bedroom. Even the unsightly cardboard box that contained my clothes had disappeared. My dresses hung neatly in the half-opened closet. Was it selfish, I wondered in my not-quite-fully-awake state, to feel so happy?

Again my Grandmother's concerned voice came from downstairs, "Ingrid, are you awake? It's soon time to go to classes. I have your breakfast ready."

I jumped out of bed as the wonderful reality of several miraculous events in my life hit me.

In the spring of 1939 I had graduated from the eighth grade at the Blackman one-room country school in Springfield. An intense desire filled my heart to go away to school in Wahoo, Nebraska, instead of the local high school that my brothers attended. I had heard about Luther Academy from my grandmother who lived in Wahoo and from my father who had graduated from there. Our Swedish forefathers founded this unique Christian high school and junior college based on a solid liberal arts curriculum patterned after the European Gymnasium model. I had already dreamed of going to the mission field and thought that this school would be the best preparation for my future.

When I told my parents how much I wanted to go, they shook their heads sadly. "We would love to make it possible for you, dear daughter, but the expense exceeds what we can give you. It is a private school that requires tuition," Daddy explained. "And besides, it is four hundred miles away from Springfield."

Trying not to show my disappointment, I looked down at the floor. After supper I fled to my old friend, the oak tree, and sat quietly for a long time, looking west into the beautiful sunset. It felt good to dig my back into the rough bark and physically draw strength from the tree's steadfast presence. Almost unconsciously, I began reciting a verse I had learned by heart during confirmation class. "If, in my name you ask me for anything, I will do it," Jesus had told his friends. I repeated the words again. And again. I prayed that I might be able to go to Luther. Every evening from then on I went to my safe place and repeated my prayer.

Several weeks went by. No sign of an answer to my prayer. I had learned how to sew in 4-H Club. Hour after hour my feet pedaled the old Singer sewing machine. My mother had entrusted me with the family mending that summer vacation. I also spent time working on my fall wardrobe, remodeling the skirts and dresses which an older cousin had given me, since I knew there would be no money for new clothes. As I finished each garment, I carefully packed it into a cardboard box under my bed in the Girls' Cottage.

July and August went by. It was the first week of September and time for the new school year to begin. Nothing had happened. I kept praying and hoping. The first day of school had already arrived. As I looked out the front door, I saw the mailman stop and put something in our big mailbox where my father had carefully printed in large letters,

> *Rev. Ralph D. Hult*
> *Route 9, Box 149-B*
> *Springfield, Missouri*

I sped down the maple lane, opened the door of the mailbox, took out the packet of mail, and ran with it to my father. He and Mother were having their morning cup of coffee together. I watched as he carefully sorted the letters. He held up and first opened a letter from his brother Martin in Wahoo. A smile spread across his face as he read it out loud: "Would you consider letting Ingrid come and live with her grandmother this year? Our mother is 75 and shouldn't be living alone anymore because of her heart condition. Ingrid could go to Luther Academy..." Uncle Martin even enclosed a ten dollar bill to cover the gasoline for the 400 mile trip!

"We need to get Ingrid's things ready," Mother said.

I smiled and proudly showed her the boxes already packed. That very afternoon my father and I started out for Wahoo in the old family car, a 1927 black Packard with noble lines. It had been the favorite car of one of my mother's aunts. When she died, her husband, instead of keeping it in his garage, gave it to us.

I quickly dressed in grandmother's house, in my very first room of my own. I relived that moment of unbelievable joy and complete happiness when, barely two days ago, we drove down our maple-lined driveway in Springfield. God had answered my prayers—another lesson in faith—as I thought back to the time we counted out the apple money in my father's silver cup. I did not remember shedding any tears as I said goodbye to Mother and hugged my brothers and sisters. Daddy and I drove and talked through the night. My joyful anticipation kept me from sleep. No wonder Grandmother had to wake me this morning! Yesterday my father had already enrolled me at the Academy. I was even awarded a scholarship covering my tuition! Today was to be my first day in class. Thoughts kept racing through my head as I laced up my new saddle shoes and tried to remain calm. Finally I half-bounced, half-skipped down the steps to Grandmother's breakfast table. I could barely contain my elation.

Homesickness was definitely not my problem that first year. Sometimes I felt guilty because I did not miss my family more. Everything had its place in Grandmother's cozy Victorian house. It felt like a little bit of heaven to me, and I reflected on the fact that there certainly would be no disorder in heaven.

"Order is the space we need for beauty."
~Pearl S. Buck~

Although my own mother tried to keep a tidy home, she could not help being overwhelmed by the sheer volume of her housekeeping and child-rearing chores. Now 400 miles removed me from my own internal pressures to help her and ease her life. Little did I realize then how deliberately and unselfishly she had let me go. In her wisdom she foresaw that my absence would give the younger siblings a chance to move up in their helping roles. She never expressed this in words to me, but I understand now how much she herself had longed to give me a broader perspective of life and the opportunity to explore my own gifts. In Wahoo I had a room and a grandmother and my own schedule that I had to share with no one else. It was the first and last time in my life that I would enjoy those three together at the same time.

I must have puzzled my teachers at the Luther Academy. Well over a year younger than most of my classmates, I was definitely ahead of them in life experience. "Ingrid, you reminded me of a little adult when you came to Luther," one of my professors told me years later.

Time alone with my grandmother became my greatest joy. Years later I was asked to write about the woman who was my role model.[2] It took me only minutes to choose her, Johanna Mathilda Lind Hult, my father's mother. There was something about her quiet strength that reminded me of Swedish steel that can stand up under great pressure. She had learned to walk alone. She did it with "strength and dignity, laughing at the days to come" (Prov. 31:25). We shared the deep joy of kinship and mutual understanding that comes from being related on both a physical and spiritual level. I marveled at her hidden strength and wanted nothing more than to be a woman like her.

Soon I realized that what I admired in her was not the result of a life of ease. Together with her mother and four siblings, she had made the long ocean voyage from her familiar Swedish homeland to the United States. Mathilda was eight years old. Her father had gone over two years earlier only to be swindled out of the first passage fares he had saved for his family through backbreaking labor in the coalmines. Finally reunited, they decided to go further west and stake out a homestead not far from Kearney in central Nebraska.

"I remember my father dropping to his knees after plowing the first furrow on our new land," Grandmother said. "He took a handful of the rich black earth, and holding it up, he praised God that there was not a stone in it bigger than a pea."

We also talked about Grandmother's first love, a handsome seminary student who died unexpectedly of tuberculosis before they could even publicly speak of their mutual friendship. A few years later she became engaged to my grandfather, Henry Edward Hult, while seated on the front steps of the church after the Sunday evening service.

With loving pride she told me about my father's birth a year after they were married, "Ingrid, dear child, I dedicated your father to God already in the womb and prayed that he would become a pastor." Quietly her hands went back to their knitting. She exuded a kind of peace that was nothing short of contagious. The space we shared together in her home became holy space.

"The core message of Jesus is that real joy and peace can never be reached while bypassing suffering and death, but only by going right through them."
~Henri Nouwen~

The rest of her story I knew. Her husband Henry was violently thrown out of his wagon by a team of runaway horses that he had borrowed in order to sell the first fruits of his harvest, the proceeds of a load of wheat, to give missions. Henry died a few days later of internal injuries. At the age of forty-three she became a widow with eight children to raise. Within one year she lost her husband, her fifteen-year-old son Milton, and her brother John who as a bachelor had come to help her. My father, her oldest child, was only eighteen and had just begun his studies at Luther Academy after helping his father on the farm for three years.

Years later, at a family reunion, I talked to one of my cousins who remembered how his grandfather had helped my grandmother after her losses. I told him I couldn't recall my father ever making a negative remark about one of his relatives.

"Of course not," my cousin said, "That was the unspoken Lind rule: You never bad-mouth your relatives."

From then on—by example—I tried to teach my children the same lesson.

"Every negative remark is a prayer to the devil."
~Walter Trobisch~

My teachers at Luther were planting for the long run. They challenged me to ask new questions and never ridiculed my initial shyness and my first attempts at writing. I still read voraciously and was extremely grateful for private piano lessons. In the school yearbook, one teacher wrote:

Any teacher can fill water pots in the class before him, but only the Master can change the water into wine. Not until the truth we teach enters the warm, rich stream of the learner's experience can we truly say that Christian education has reached its goal. To make life rich and abundant, is our aim at this school—not just filling the brain and training the intellect.

How privileged I was to have such devoted teachers. I think of Gladys Peterson who was my psychology professor. After I graduated from Luther, I didn't see Miss Gladys again for more than 40 years. When I visited her home in Lindsborg, Kansas, she took me in her bedroom and there on the mirror of her dresser was my high school graduation picture. "I have prayed for you daily these many years," she said, "and now I see that God has answered my prayers."

In the meantime, Europe was embroiled in World War II. In 1941, before the United States was at war with Germany, the German raider Atlantis sank the supposedly neutral Egyptian liner *Zamzam* in the South Atlantic. On board the vessel were more than 120 missionaries; my father was among them.

Why had he gone back to Africa after serving at home for more than a decade? Out of the blue in January 1941 he had received a letter from the Augustana Lutheran Church Board of Missions. There was a great need in the orphaned mission fields of East Africa. Because of the war, many German missionaries had been interned or deported. In cautious tones Dr. Hjalmar Swanson, our mission director, asked Ralph Hult, now fifty-two and the father of ten, if he would consider returning to Tanzania for the duration of the emergency.

Inwardly, he must have been tormented. He knew only too well what it would mean if he said yes—separation, not only from his wife, but also from his growing children who needed a father. Wouldn't the price of answering the call be too great? Yet, how could he stay at home when he had been summoned to help?

"If you plant for one year, you plant rice.
If you plant for ten years, you plant a tree.
If you plant for a hundred years, you educate."
~Chinese proverb~

Two great emotional experiences stand out in my memory during my years at Luther, both having to do with my father.

May 19, 1941. I was a sophomore and just leaving my Latin II class when the college president stopped me on the stair landing of Old Main. "Come into my office, Ingrid. There is something I must tell you."

I followed him. Both the tone of his voice and troubled look on his kindly face alarmed me. Had something happened to one of my brothers or sisters? To my mother? I remembered a conversation with my best friend Phyllis just a few days earlier.

"What would be the most terrible thing that could happen to you right now?" she had asked me.

With no hesitation I blurted out, "That something might happen to my father on his trip to Africa." That must be it, I thought. Something has happened to my father.

Then I saw Uncle Martin standing at the door of the President's office. After we were seated, Dr. Lindberg told me in quiet, deliberate words: "We've just heard on the radio that the *Zamzam* has been sunk by a German raider. They're afraid everyone on board is lost."

The *Zamzam*—my father's ship! He had sailed on it from New York to go back to East Africa. And we had been waiting every day for a cable telling of his safe arrival in Capetown. The *Zamzam* was long overdue.

The United States was not yet at war with Germany. Why would Germany sink a neutral ship with women and children on board and all those missionaries hoping to get back to their fields in Africa?

My father dead? Somehow in my heart I couldn't believe it. I felt certain he was still alive. I looked at Dr. Lindberg. "Are you sure?"

He nodded. I could see by his face that he believed it. But I couldn't—at least not yet.

"You are excused from classes the rest of the day, Ingrid." He said gently.

As I went to get my books, I thought of Mother back home on the farm in Springfield, Missouri. How would she be taking the news? I hurried to my grandmother's house two blocks away. This would be a hard blow for her. My father, her oldest son, was not the only one on the *Zamzam* who was dear to her. Her daughter Ida was also on board with her doctor husband, Dr. Einar Norberg, and their three children.

As I walked up the steps, I was conscious of the inviting porch swing, the lace curtains, the potted plants in every window. I opened the front door and stepped into the hallway onto the braided rug. A rush of memories overwhelmed me, and I felt a tightness in my throat. I was standing on the very spot where I had said good-bye to Daddy just three months earlier.

Grandmother was sitting in her rocking chair, close to the radio. The sunshine was streaming across her prized plants— the Crown of Thorns, a red begonia, and the geraniums which I can still smell.

Her face was calm. She was just being quiet, a discipline acquired with difficulty during her seventy-seven years, for she was an energetic little woman, always busy. Her hair was still black except for a few strands of gray above her temples. She wore her favorite brown wool dress with her amethyst necklace. There were no tears in her eyes.

I put my hand over hers. She responded in silent understanding. I felt that she too had hope. Expressions of sympathy or comfort were unnecessary.

Her words of farewell to my father came back to me. With her head barely even with his shoulder, she had looked up at him and said, "Ralph, remember when you left for Africa the first time more than twenty years ago? I told you that it was the happiest day of my life. Today I want to say the same thing."

Now the radio was telling her that she had lost not only a son, but also a daughter and all her daughter's family. Yet she sat there calm and controlled.

I heard a car stop in front of the house. A man with a big camera bag slung over his shoulder hurried up the steps.

"I'm from the Herald in Omaha," he said. "I'd like to interview Mrs. Hult, please. The sinking of the *Zamzam* is headline news all over the nation," he said to her. "I have the passenger list here. Is it true that you had both a son and a daughter on board?"

Grandmother nodded and told him to sit down. She answered his questions without a tremor.

"Why did Ralph Hult want to go to Africa when he knew it would be so dangerous?" the reporter asked.

"Let me read to you a few lines from his last letter," she said,

"'We are not going out on an adventure trip. This is a matter of urgent business for the Kingdom of God. Why should

we not be confident? In giving His disciples the great commission, our Savior assured them, 'Behold, I am with you always.'"

The reporter asked permission to take a picture. I was to
pose turning the dial of the table radio while my grandmother
listened. The picture appeared on the front page of the New
York Herald Tribune later that day.

But what about Daddy? Was he really lost at sea? I remembered just the week before how I had heard my relatives
talking about him in my grandmother's living room while I
was doing my homework in the next room. They did not
know I could hear their concerned words as to why he should
go to Africa during these dangerous days. Wasn't his ship
long overdue in reaching Capetown? I hid in the closet under
the stairs where my grandmother kept her Southern Comfort,
her vacuum sweeper, and the leaves for her oak dining table. I
had thrown myself down on the stack of Life magazines and
wept in great shaking sobs. Didn't they understand that he
had to go back to Africa and that we were behind his decision
to go? He would never have gone if Mother had not encouraged him, knowing the great need. I did not creep out of my
hiding place until everyone had left.

In retrospect I realize now that many in his generation and
even I had been taught that a call to the mission field ranked
above the immediate needs of family and marriage. The
earthly sacrifice of leaving wife and children was justified
when obeying the call to higher service. After all, could anyone accuse the missionary of following his own selfish ambi-
tion? Or of dreaming his own selfish dream? For many years
my younger brothers struggled with the feeling of being
abandoned by their father, a feeling I never shared because I
understood his burning desire to go where God wanted him
to be, no matter what the emotional cost. Of course, as one
of the older children, I also had more memories of good
times with my father than did my younger siblings. Perhaps it
was easier for me to let him go.

Of course, Daddy had asked Mother and us children how we felt. There was no doubt in our hearts that he should go on this journey for what we thought would be a temporary situation.

My father wired his acceptance to the mission board. He was to be in New York by March 10th and ready to sail soon thereafter. He applied for his passport. In Springfield he bought and packed khaki outfits for the tropics, mosquito nets, cooking utensils, and medicines. He painted his initials, R D H, in neat letters on his steel footlockers.

In February he had come to Wahoo to bid his mother, his brothers and sisters, and his oldest daughter good-bye.

How I loved him with the single-heartedness of a young daughter's devotion as I saw him walking toward me with his tall, erect figure and his purposeful stride!

His hair had been gray as long as I could remember, for he had seen much suffering. The wrinkles around his kind and gentle eyes made him look as if he were always smiling. Yet, in the determined set of his mouth and chin, there was no compromise.

Now, coping with the news, I thought of Mother back home in Missouri. What kind of a day was she having? A wave of homesickness overcame me. All of a sudden I knew what I needed. To see my mother, my brothers and sisters, to go to my safe place and hidden refuge. To feel the strength of the oak tree behind me as I drank in the view of the rolling Ozark hills which always rejoiced and strengthened me.

The woods would be changing from the first delicate green of spring to the full, rich green of May. Standing out against the green would be the lavender red of the redbud trees, the rosy pink of the wild crabapple blossoms. All the fruit trees would be in bloom, and their fragrance would permeate the air.

I heard steps on the front porch. Someone entered without knocking. It was my Uncle Les, clasping a bouquet of gladiolas. Silently, with tears in his eyes, he held them out to me.

I welcomed his embrace of sympathy and his loving concern, but my heart was crying, "Why is he doing this? This is what people do when a loved one is dead. But my father is not dead—I know he's not. Neither are my aunt and uncle, nor my cousins and the other passengers aboard the *Zamzam*." We turned on the radio for the next news report. It was the same.

The day dragged on. We listened to the evening news which brought a thin ray of hope. If any passengers survived, they could have been taken aboard a prison ship. Was my father among them?

May 19, 1941—the longest day I had lived through. I didn't expect to sleep that night, but I must have done so. The next thing I knew, the phone was ringing.

I picked up the receiver and heard the operator say: "Long distance calling."

Then I heard an unfamiliar voice. "This is Dr. Swanson calling from Mission headquarters. We've just received good news from the United Press. Your father is alive and safe. So are all the other missionaries and passengers. Will you tell your grandmother and mother?"

It was no longer Black Monday, but Tuesday the 20th. The sun was shining. Birds were singing. The world went round and round, full of Easter joy.

I called Mother back home in Springfield.

"Yes, I know," she replied calmly. "Our neighbor spent all night at his short-wave set. He brought me the good news early this morning. They're safe in a German-occupied port in France."

We later learned that, for thirty days and thirty nights, the passengers of the *Zamzam* had been on the *Dresden*, a German prison ship, and that they had run the British blockade in constant danger of being torpedoed.

The American passengers were allowed to go to neutral Portugal, and from there the State Department arranged their repatriation. My father was one of the last to leave, hoping against hope for passage to Africa.

The day of his homecoming in Springfield was celebrated to the fullest. On Sunday evening we gathered in the living room, putting our chairs in a circle, our family tradition. We sang our evening hymn *Day is Dying in the West*. Then Daddy told us about his feelings as he initially left the New York harbor on March 20th.

> *Darkness was gathering as we glided down the Hudson River and past the Statue of Liberty. It was a historic moment. Your Aunt Ida was standing beside me. 'Ralph,' she said, 'from the look on your face, I think you must be the happiest man on board.' 'Yes,' I answered, 'I believe I am. If only Gertrude and the children were at my side, my fulfillment would be complete.'*

Little did he know what he would be facing in the weeks and months ahead. God brought him home again to us before he would reach his beloved Africa and be buried there.

I never went back to my grandmother's house, nor did I have my own room again. My family needed me. Something, however, had begun to change inside me. I needed my own space less and less for personal happiness, security, and shelter. My first lessons in faith and in answered prayer had begun to build up sturdy walls around the chamber of my heart. This new inner room and sanctuary was one I could at all times carry within me, even to the strangest corners of the earth.

"Make two homes for thyself,
...one actual home
...and another spiritual home,
which thou are to carry with thee always."
~Catherine of Sienna~

My heart was filled with the assurance of a call to follow my father's example and to serve God wherever He might send me and whatever the cost. I had started to trust in a new way, and I was willing to live in whatever space God saw fit for me. I had learned to rely on God even when I didn't understand Him.

Walter at Augustana Seminary

Ingrid boarding the Rock Island Rocket

FOUR

ANCHORED IN LOVE

"Only he who keeps his eyes fixed on the far horizon
will find the right road."
~Dag Hammarskjöld~

After his fateful trip on the *Zamzam* and another year of
waiting, my father had returned to Africa in June 1942. By
that time the United States had entered World War II, and
any ocean voyage was dangerous. He traveled with his fellow
missionary Ludwig Melander on a secret munitions convoy to
South Africa. From there he made the long trip inland to
Tanzania. He wrote to Mother from their old home near
Moshi:

> *It is a thrill to come back after so many years and find African*
> *Christians who still remember us. Every time I go in and out of this*
> *house, I am reminded of days gone by.*
>
> *The first thing I did after I arrived here was to visit the cemetery*
> *and to stand there beside our precious little grave. I imagined you at*
> *my side, dear Gertrude-wife, and I asked you all the questions in my*
> *heart… How different everything would be for me now if we could*
> *have carried on in Africa together all these years. Why should we*
> *have been cut off from the tasks we so much loved… I hope and pray*
> *that we still have something to do in the missionary work of today.*
> *And where our work shall end, may our children carry on.*

Father was stationed at Dar-es-Salaam, the capital of Tanzania and one of its main ports. Dar was considered a hardship post, for the climate was hot and humid, and at that time disease was rampant. Father did not mind, so great was his happiness to be at work in his beloved Africa. He wrote:

> *I have arrived at Dar at the beginning of the hot season," he wrote us. "You can imagine how I perspire in this sticky heat.... Even at night it is hot and one never wakens refreshed. I walk to the waterfront early in the morning and late in the evening. It is so refreshing to get even slight breezes from off the water... At times I'm almost sick with my longing to see you and be with you. It's now five months since the last letter I received from you was written.*

That made our hearts ache, for we had faithfully answered each one of his letters. My two younger sisters, Veda and Eunice, were now with me at Luther Academy in Wahoo, Nebraska. We all lived in the girls' dormitory.

On March 23rd in 1943 I was resting between classes in my room. In a few minutes the bell would ring for our ten o'clock period. Suddenly I heard a knock at the door.

"Come in," I called, without bothering to get up. I was startled to see Pastor Lauersen, our new president, standing in the doorway. I was even more alarmed when I saw that Veda and Eunie were with him. Why should he be here in the girls' dorm? What was wrong?

In a flash I thought of that other Monday morning just two years ago when Dr. Lindberg had told me the news of the sinking of the *Zamzam*. What would it be this time? I felt it even before he told us.

President Lauersen was solemn. "I wanted you girls to be all together before I say what I have to say," he declared. "A cablegram has just been received from Dar-es-Salaam. Your father passed away from heart failure following malaria on March 18th." He had broken it to us as gently as he could.

That other time I had said to myself, "I know my father is not dead. He is alive. I will see him again." But this time I knew with a great finality that my father was dead. That was the greatest blow of my young life.

Veda and Eunie wept almost hysterically at the first shock of the news. But as we fell into each other's arms, we knew a great comfort, a comfort from outside ourselves.

Pastor Lauersen continued, "Your mother down in Springfield, alone with your five youngest brothers and sisters, has not heard. You're the one who must tell her, Ingrid."

I called Mother at the Bethany Homestead. She answered the phone and greeted me with her usual cheeriness.

"Mother," I said, "I have some bad news for you."

"Yes, Ingrid, tell me what it is," she said slowly.

I read her the cablegram we had received from the mission office. There was a long moment of silence. Then she asked me in a normal voice how we were.

The word of my father's death had a great impact on the student body. Pastor Lauersen told the news to one of the college classes. A hushed silence followed. "It was here that Pastor Hult first heard the call to Africa and dedicated his life to becoming a missionary. Now he is dead. Who will carry on where he left off?"

Ten of the young men in that class raised their hands and came forward while the others bowed their heads in prayer. Of those ten, seven would become missionaries, the other three, pastors here at home.

A few days later my mother wrote to her family:

I thank God from the depths of my soul that Ralph was permitted to return to Africa for at least a few months. God has especially blessed me in giving me the love of a man with such a deep abiding faith in His Master... The future does not look dark to me because I am confident that God's promise to be with us always will be fulfilled.

When she came to Wahoo for his memorial service, I tried to think of some way to comfort her. She answered me simply, "You do not yet realize, Ingrid, what it means to lose your life partner."

During the memorial service I had the strong sense that Father had found peace at last in the continent he loved. I stood up and announced with a trembling voice: "My brothers and sisters and I are now more determined than ever that we want to give our lives entirely to the expansion of God's kingdom here on earth, in the manner and place which to Him seems best."

It is difficult to find words for my own spiritual awakening. I remember the summer of 1944, the year after my father's death. I had finished my first year of college and took a summer job as a parish assistant in Minneapolis at Trinity Lutheran Church of Minnehaha Falls. Those three months changed my life. I grasped in a new way that God had no grandchildren. Just because my parents were God's children, did not mean that I automatically had a special relationship with God. My parents could not communicate with Him for me. I had to learn to do it myself.

The loud voices of friends and family had also begun to crowd out Christ's quiet, persistent voice in my heart. I was deeply convicted by St. Augustine's words, "He who loves not Christ above all, loves not Christ at all." I was not letting Christ come first in my life.

"Aim at heaven and you get earth thrown in;
aim at earth and you get neither."
~C.S. Lewis~

Deep dissatisfaction with myself seemed to spoil any joy in things around me. No matter how hard I tried, I never could live up to the standards that I knew Christ had set for me. My attempts at being pure and blameless seemed futile. Finally and suddenly, God's word broke open my heart like a hammer. I was stunned by the revelation that faith was not something I had to produce. Faith was a free gift. All I had to do was hold out my empty hand. The reality and existence of Christ's love in my life did not depend on my behavior. He loved me unconditionally, no strings attached. His love was simply there, and His love, in turn, transformed me.

Stones lifted from my heart. I clung to Paul's saying, "If any (wo)man is in Christ, (s)he is a new creature." I repeated the blind man's awestruck acknowledgment, "Once I was blind, but now I see." For the first time in my life I publicly spoke in church of these new truths I had learned. I thought I would burst if I couldn't share the incredible sense of freedom and weightlessness that had spread in my heart.

Years before, I had chosen to follow in the footsteps of my father. I suppose there was something quite romantic about going to Africa (via Paris!) as an eligible and unattached young woman. God, however, still had some dramatic inward readjustments to make before I was ready to serve Him in His way. Many times I stumbled because of my own stubbornness during those college years. Slowly, ever so slowly, I learned to pray, "Not my will, but thy will be done."

I had graduated from Augustana College in Rock Island, Illinois, where both of my parents had graduated. I then took special training at our missions institute in Minneapolis. This included practical courses in childbirth as well as tropical medicine and linguistics. I applied and was accepted by the Sudan Mission, a Lutheran faith mission, to work as a missionary teacher in French Cameroun, West Africa. I wanted to go where my father had longed to do pioneer work, but he was unable to do so because of his mission board's decision to concentrate their work in East Africa.

I needed $2,000 for a year of language study in Paris and transportation to Africa. "God will provide," William Berg, my pastor, mentor, and fatherly friend said. He posted the list of some 300 items which I would need—lanterns, a coffee grinder, a gristmill, a meat saw, and various tools. Without any campaign, every item arrived. The missionary's *outfit* was now being packed in the basement of the church.

"Before you sail for France on February 17, the $2,000 will be here," Pastor Berg said confidently. "It's like a miracle. For such a cause, you do not need to plead; what is needed comes from heaven."

A boy from a children's home, a former delinquent, sent 50 cents with the message: "Hope this will help you get to Africa."

And then came the moment of my commissioning service, January 23, 1949. On that evening I sensed my father's gentle presence. Almost seven years had gone by since he had given me that last hug in Springfield. His patient teaching and example had made it but a tiny step of faith to find my heavenly Father. I had learned to find shelter seated on His lap and let myself be loved. The *awareness of belovedness*, as Brennan Manning puts it, became real to me.

Never before had I seen the church so full as the evening I walked slowly down the center aisle of the familiar sanctuary of First Lutheran Church in Rock Island, Illinois. Again the simplicity and warmth of the worship space struck me. The wooden pews stood in pleasing contrast to the rich crimson carpeting and white communion rail. The altar painting of Jesus praying in Gethsemane focused the eyes and attention of everyone present. There was standing room only after the ushers brought in folding chairs. Dr. Conrad Bergendoff, a close friend of my parents and president of Augustana College and Seminary, sat in the front row. Across the aisle from him were six of my brothers and sisters. A special place next to them had been saved for me.

When Pastor Berg called my name, I confidently walked up to the altar and knelt, remembering my promise at my father's memorial service six years earlier. Mission Director Gunderson and several local pastors laid their hands in blessing on my head and shoulders. I also was keenly aware that my older brother John, a senior at Washington University Medical School, had stepped up behind me and placed his hand on my head. When I thanked him later he said, "That wasn't my hand—it was the hand of our father."

A sea of love surrounded me. For months and years later I clung to the reality of that evening's solemn ceremony. I remembered the faithful people who cared for me and who had promised to pray for my protection and safety. Walter Trobisch, a German exchange student, was in the audience, as well as Lauren Youngdale, a future pastor.

It was like the Lord had put me on a slide, and the closer I got to my goal, the more the momentum carried me. There was no turning back. Yes, just as Pastor Berg said, the $2,000 miraculously materialized. That still did not make it easy to leave my home base.

"I feel as though I am being let down in a pit," I told my friends in church on the last Sunday. "I'm so glad to know that you are here, praying and holding the ropes."

I boarded the 10:30 Rock Island Rocket for Chicago on a Monday morning. As my train pulled out of the station, I watched the faithful group, who had come to see me off, recede in the distance. Real to me was the long, long rope being unwound with each mile the train sped on its way. The end of the rope was secure.

"Happiness is essentially a state of going somewhere, wholeheartedly, one-directionally, without regret or reservation."
~William H. Sheldon~

On February 17, 1949, I awoke early in my pleasant, single room at the Lutheran Home for Women on 3rd and 82nd Street in New York City. After years of dreaming, waiting, and hard preparation, I had reached my goal. It was my twenty-third birthday. I closed and labeled the copper-belted trunk that would be my symbol of home for the next decades in Europe and Africa. Not for 33 years would this sturdy trunk return to America, filled with a few precious possessions from my homes abroad.

I sat at the desk in my room, ready to write words of farewell to my mother who was now 50. After learning Spanish, she had gone to Bolivia with my two youngest siblings, Mary and David. She served as matron of an orphanage near La Paz.

"This business of getting the Gospel to the ends of the world is so important that even we grandmothers have to go," she had said clearly at her commissioning service two years earlier. My oldest brother Paul and his wife had just had their first child. Mother had written me, "Time has never gone faster for me than this year. I do love my work so much and am so thankful to be here."

My sister Mary, age 12, had written at Christmas, "I have something wonderful to tell you. Since I came to Bolivia, I have found my Savior. I wanted Him all the time, but didn't want to confess my sins. When I finally gave in, and told Him all the stuff I wasn't proud of and didn't want Mother to know, something wonderful happened. Now I'm very happy."

I sat at the desk in my room and picked up our church paper, The Lutheran Companion (February 9, 1949). I saw the editorial by E.E. Ryden: "Takes up Father's Torch" and the lead article entitled: "Dream of Ralph Hult Realized in Children." I read it again:

The story of the Hult family is full of drama. It began with the call that came to the 18-year-old Nebraska boy when, as a student at Luther Academy, he heard of the spiritual need of the Sudan tribes. His hopes seemed to give promise of beautiful fulfillment when the Augustana Synod in 1917 agreed to ordain him and to commission him as its first missionary to Africa. The entry of the United States into World War I brought the first interruption to his plans, but two years later he was able to leave for Africa.

A romantic touch was added to the story in 1921 when his young bride, two years after their marriage, bravely set out alone to join her husband in the interior of Africa. Accompanied only by native guides, she penetrated the jungles on foot and by riverboats until she finally reached her husband, deep in the heart of West Africa.

Then followed the strange sequence of events by which the orphaned German mission fields in Tanganyika, East Africa, were "adopted" by Augustana Church and the Hults were ordered to leave West Africa and to begin work in the new field. To Ralph Hult this proved a bitter disappointment, and he was never able to reconcile himself to the fact that he had not kept his promise to the Sara tribe to return to that region.

After his return to America, there followed years of shattered dreams and frustrated hopes. With a family of ten children, the economic situation at times became acute, especially during the weary depression years.

When finally another World War brought a second crisis to the German missions in Tanganyika and a call went forth for emergency volunteers, Ralph Hult was one of those who answered. Once more, however, it seemed as though some strange fate were pursuing him when the SS Zamzam on which he sailed was sunk by a German raider and tragedy was narrowly averted. Instead of reaching Africa, he landed in a prison ship and was finally returned to America. It was all of another year before he saw the shores of his beloved Africa, and then only for a brief while. Before a year was gone, the eager, zealous soul of Ralph Hult had found peace at last, and the heart that had always yearned for Africa was at rest beneath the palm trees of Dar-es-Salaam, in the soil of the continent he loved.

It now appears that his life-long dream for the Sudan, unfulfilled in his own life, will be realized through his children. When Ingrid Hult was commissioned as a missionary on January 13, six of her brothers and sisters who are still in school participated in the service. It was not only impressive, but gripping...

Slowly the words for the letter to my mother formed themselves: "Mother, the last chapter hasn't been written yet about Daddy's and your life in Africa. It's wonderful to see now how the prayers and heartaches of thirty and more years are bearing fruit. I find that the story of Daddy's death in Africa touches hearts, but even more so does the story of your obedience to God's call in Bolivia…"

I was interrupted by a knock at the door. It was Mrs. Karlson, the matron, who told me that my taxi had arrived. As my overseas baggage was loaded into the large taxi, she wished me a safe voyage.

It was only a short ride to Pier 61 on North River, where the *SS America* was berthed and proudly receiving her passengers for LeHavre, France. I looked up at the elegant ship over 700 feet long with staterooms and cabins for more than a thousand passengers. For months I had looked forward to this moment as I had saved the $200 for my tourist class ticket. I stood in line for the customs formalities with my new passport and ticket in hand.

My yellow vaccination card issued by the US Department of Health was checked. Smallpox, yellow fever, cholera, typhus, and tetanus shots—I had endured them all. My baggage, marked with my cabin number, was taken away by a porter. Cranes were still loading provisions and the large trunks into the hold.

A steady stream of passengers walked up the two gangplanks, one for the first class and the other for tourist class. Without looking back, I stepped from the swaying gangplank onto the ship that would take me to Europe. There was no turning back. I had made a choice. In the years ahead I would experience love, joy and sorrow, and birth and death, before I would return to my homeland.

I wore a long, free-flowing gray woolen coat with a dark green beret perched on my wavy auburn hair. Not for 33 years would this sturdy trunk return to America, filled with a few precious possessions from my homes abroad. Slung around my neck was my new 35mm Argus camera, enclosed in the brown leather carrying case which my father had used.

The band was playing as we stood on the deck, and people waved from the pier. A uniformed bellboy paraded up and down the corridors, using a Chinese gong and saying to the visitors on board, "All ashore that's going ashore." And then came the ship's whistle, an inadequate name for the shattering, majestic blast it produced. I watched as the gangplanks of the huge ship were drawn up and was again jolted by the bellowing sound of that deep-throated whistle—a sound that carried a feeling of departure, longing, and loss.

The ship began to move down the North River as the mouth of the Hudson is called. We had a magnificent view of Manhattan and the New York skyline. A few minutes later we sailed past the Statue of Liberty. I thought of Deuteronomy 32:11 where Moses speaks of the mother eagle that stirs up her nest, forcing her young ones to try their wings. I was leaving behind my siblings, my friends, and all my safe places, and I was sailing off to a new world. I knew no one on board ship, only the number of my tourist class cabin. I would find it and hide my tears.

As I searched for it down the long corridors, a smartly uniformed bellboy came by, paging someone as he rang his little bell. I listened. He was calling my name. I followed after him and touched his sleeve. He looked at me for a moment and then said, "Who are you anyway? Are you someone special? I've got some mail for you." His arms were full of letters. "There's more in the purser's office."

He looked at me curiously until I explained, "I'm a missionary on my way to Paris and then to Africa. And today's my birthday. I had almost forgotten it."

I wept, but these were tears of happiness. My friends had not forgotten me.

One encouraging letter was from Pastor Berg. He wrote:

Happy Birthday! I have the feeling that this is the finest and happiest birthday of your life. If you could fully realize how many fervent prayers are reaching the Throne of Grace on your behalf today, your joy would be as boundless as the ocean wide upon which you sail... Your life has been gloriously full and fruitful, but the best is yet ahead.

This Sunday I preached on the parable of the Laborers in the Vineyard. Remember how the first workers bargained with the householder in Matt. 20:2. But the next ones trusted him when he said, 'Go... and whatsoever is right, I will give you.'

Later in the letter, Pastor Berg wrote, "You trust and He will provide."

---

*"The supreme happiness in life is the conviction
that we are loved."*
~Victor Hugo~

The crossing was smooth, and I spent hours in a deck chair, looking back as well as ahead. Several times my thoughts went back to a graduate German exchange student, Walter Trobisch, whom I knew only casually. We had sat in the college cafeteria together with several friends. He had told us of his carefree childhood and of the grim war years in Germany. I could not forget his editorial in our college newspaper:

You Americans have to remember that God is not a Santa Claus, not an old grandpa walking around in his bath-robe with an ever smiling face, always ready to reward us for good behavior, and always glad when we say to Him a gracious 'Thank you'! If He wants to, He can destroy everything and everybody you know.

Walter spoke from the depths of his heart. At the age of 18 he had been drafted into Hitler's army, had been wounded several times during the war and had lost his only sister. He saw the fate of Germany as a warning sign to the nations of the world. When he spoke, he disarmed me with his quiet and intense convictions. Around him I felt like my faith had become too simple and complacent.

Little did I realize that he had attended my commissioning service, standing at the very back of the church. Later that night he was to write in his journal: Sunday, January 23, 1949:

Cleaned my room. Went to the service at First Lutheran for Miss Ingrid Hult. She's 22. Clear, committed, ready for any battle, and yet every inch a woman. Such a person I would marry without a moment's hesitation.

And then he forgot that he had ever written it. It was more than 40 years later, long after his death, while leafing through his journals, that I discovered the entry the German student had made that night.

"The world is a book.
The one who stays home sees only one page."
~St. Augustine~

Paris was indeed a new page in my life. I found an ideal room just a stone's throw from the Luxembourg Garden. My landlady was a doctor, and we soon became friends. Through Dr. Tisserand I learned to appreciate the French mind which greatly values clarity and precision. One author has said, "That which is not easily understood is not French."

My room was actually the maid's room under the roof, called a *mansard* in French, and rather cold. I did have a little electric heater, but each time I plugged it in, the fuse blew out, so I just kept warm by putting on layers of clothing. I described it to my sister Martha:

I wish you could see my cute little room. I can turn around twice in it—but it's cozy with a couch that serves as a bed and a desk, above which I have my bookshelves filled with French study books and pictures of my family. It's on the 7th floor and has a window with a southern exposure that supposedly means I get the sun every time it decides to shine. This time of year that isn't too often.

There's a coffee roasting shop down below and with it the smell of burnt chicory which the French use in their coffee. On my desk is Fa-

ther's carved wooden cross given to him by an African chief and which he always kept on his desk at home.

I hope by now you've received the little package I mailed about 3 weeks ago. You're probably wondering why the steel bookends are enclosed. Please do me a favor, Martha. Can you take the bookends back to the Luther College library where they belong? I took them six years ago and have had them ever since. When I examined my conscience and asked myself if everything I have really belongs to me, I couldn't say yes because of these. I'm enclosing a note for the librarian. Thanks so much, dear sister.

I faithfully attended classes at the Alliance Francaise and also at the Sorbonne. After a year I obtained both my Diplome Moyen and Diplome Superieure. One more diploma and I would be certified to teach French in any country of the world outside of France. In the midst of this daily routine I received a letter from the young German I had met briefly in the States a year earlier.

Walter Trobisch was now serving as a youth minister in Ludwigshafen, Germany. He invited me to come and talk to his youth groups about my call to become a missionary. I promptly declined his invitation. I had far too many things to do before leaving for Africa. Making a trip to Germany was not one of them.

A few days later, during our geography class, the professor announced we would have a week's vacation because of Mardi Gras. What would I do with those days? I looked at the map of France and saw that Ludwigshafen was not far from the French-German border. Why not go there after all? I wrote to the young pastor and said I could accept his invitation if it was still valid. Two days later I received a telegram: "Willkommen!"

It was a strange feeling to be getting off the Paris train at gray, industrial Ludwigshafen. I kept asking myself, "What am I doing here? What would my mother think?" But now I was committed. There was Walter Trobisch, waiting for me wearing his motorcycle suit designed to keep out both wind and rain. The one-piece suit didn't exactly flatter him, I thought.

"I'm in a hurry. There is a youth meeting I have to get to," he explained casually. "My friend here will take you to the senior pastor's home where you will be staying." This offhand reception did little to warm my feelings toward him. "What was I doing here?" I wondered as his friend took me on the streetcar to Pastor Kreiselmaier's home.

The minute I entered the door, I felt better. Mrs. Kreiselmaier was as kind to me as if I were her daughter. I felt immediately at home. My American-Swedish traditions fit their lifestyle much more than the *sidewalk-café* Parisian style. She was also honest in letting me know that the military look of my U.S. army raincoat, which I purchased at the army surplus store, could send the wrong message to the people I would be talking to. She kindly offered me her best black coat for my stay in Germany.

I did not see Walter Trobisch again until the next afternoon when he showed me his one-room apartment and shared his plan for the youth gathering that evening. We would both tell our stories, and he would be my interpreter. The meeting room was packed with young people who listened with rapt attention. I sensed an unexpected blessing on our teamwork. So far our communication had been highly impersonal. It was almost as if we were getting to know each other indirectly through our audience.

After the meeting Walter asked me if I were afraid to ride with him the next day on his motorcycle. I pretended to be courageous and said yes, I would go, although I'd never been on a motorcycle in my life, let alone in the month of February when it was cold and wet.

"Good!" he said, "Then I'd like to show you the work of the Volksmission here. But it'll mean a fifty-mile ride on the back of my machine. Are you ready?"

I nodded stoically as Frau Kreiselmaier searched her daughter's closets for all the warm clothing she could find. Bundled in sweaters, ski pants, scarves and even an aviator's helmet, I took my place, not on a dashing white steed but on the back saddle of Walter's powerful, black 500 cc Horex. I was both anxious and apprehensive. Pastor Kreiselmaier looked on disapprovingly.

At first I was quietly terrified. Once we were out on the highway, I began to relax as we traveled through the quaint wine villages of the Palatinate. Sitting so closely behind Walter on his beloved motorcycle felt wonderful and inappropriate at the same time. I struggled to sort out my feelings. What kind of risky adventure was this? Soon it began to rain, followed quickly by icy sleet. More than once the motorcycle skidded.

At last we arrived at the village of Annweiler. We knocked at the door of the parsonage. The pastor's wife exclaimed in surprise when she saw the two soaked and shivering wayfarers.

"Come in quickly," she said. "Get those wet clothes off. Sit by the fire, and I'll bring you some hot water to soak your feet in."

I was embarrassed, but Walter seemed to be enjoying himself tremendously as we soaked our feet together. "What would your friends say if they could see us right now?" he teased. But he was kind. I was given a place to rest on the sofa in the pastor's study. Walter tucked a blanket carefully around my feet. His gesture touched me deeply. Only my father would have done that for me.

We heard the town crier outside. An important meeting was being announced in the village church at 7:30 p.m. Everyone was invited. Walter explained that since bombs had destroyed the Protestant Church, the only other place in town big enough for the evangelistic meeting was the Catholic Church. Pastor Fuchs and Walter would be speaking. Several lay people would also take part and tell about their journey of faith: a woman physician, a farmer, a factory worker, and a high school teacher. I felt honored to be a witness of God's moving in post-war Germany.

I shall never forget that evening. The large, unheated church was filled with expectant people, dressed in many layers to keep warm. We could actually see our breaths, so even the speakers kept their overcoats and scarves on. The audience listened attentively to each one on the team.

Then it was Walter's turn. Clad in his gray, oil-splattered motorcycle suit, he told of his colorful adventures in America. As he spoke, the audience laughed and then listened with intense interest. I understood only a few words of his German, but I could not take my eyes off him. His presence commanded the attention of everyone in that room. I heard a strong inner voice: "Ingrid, do you remember your lifelong prayer? Look, this is the one who is to be your life partner." I gasped and thought, "But he's not at all my dream image. He's barely as tall as I am, and he's a German. (In 1951 this statement was loaded.) I wanted to marry a tall Swede. He has a call to work with youth in Europe, and I'm about to go to Africa. How does that go together?"

The meeting ended. It was decided that, instead of driving back to Ludwigshafen in the cold winter night, we would wait until morning. I was to stay in the pastor's home. The pastor's wife served me cocoa and cookies that night. She spoke good English and explained that their home had been bombed during the last days of the war. It was still under repair five years later. As she showed me where I would sleep, she told me this was the room where their only daughter had been killed when American bombs fell on their village.

I didn't sleep much that night. I thought of what my father had told me when I was nine that I was not too young to pray for the one who would be my life partner. I had taken his advice seriously. Each time during my student years when I was on the verge of a deeper friendship with a young man, it was as if the Lord said, "Not yet, Ingrid. Just wait." And now this!

The next morning as we traveled on the motorcycle back to Ludwigshafen, Walter and I exchanged polite, impersonal remarks. Tomorrow I would be going back to Paris. Walter said he'd come early in the afternoon to visit before preparing for another youth meeting that evening.

"At last," I thought, "perhaps the barriers between us will be broken down." But he did not come back—not at one o'clock, nor at two o'clock, nor at three. It was four-thirty when he finally arrived to pick me up. His only explanation was that he thought I needed rest and that it would also give him a good chance to catch up on his correspondence. I was speechless and inwardly I fumed.

"What's the matter, Ingrid?" Walter asked, genuinely puzzled. "I can feel that something is bothering you. You must share your feelings with me, or else there will be no blessing on our meeting tonight."

So I poured out all that was on my mind. I accused him of using me to further his own interests. Oh, he was kind enough to me, I said, but in a way one would be kind to a little prize dog. This cold indifference—what did it mean? Why had I come at all? Why hadn't I stayed in Paris where I belonged?

Walter looked at me in amazement. First he tried to explain his attitude of seeming indifference. It was because he felt he should remain single for some years in order to be free to do the work that was so close to his heart in Germany. The doors seemed to be wide open for his ministry among youth. As a leader he had learned to be extremely careful not to stir up any personal feelings of the young women he came in contact with. At that point in time, after the ravages of the war years, there was only one man for every seven women in Germany.

Then he continued:

"Ingrid, I never meant to hurt you. I know of no young woman in whom I could be more interested than in you. But your life is so organized, so well-ordered, that if I were to enter it, I would be like an elephant in a china shop."

It was time for the evening meal and the youth meeting. Again I experienced the pure joy of being the team partner of a man who knew where he was going. He had a clear sense of guidance in all that he did.

The next day he took me to the station where I boarded the train for Paris. We agreed to be quiet before God and let Him show us the next step.

A few days later I received this note from him, penned carefully in English:

Dear Ingrid,

Thank you for speaking to our youth here. One night is over since you took leave. Something that was blocked for a long time is streaming out of my heart. I write my feelings as honestly as I can. I am still happy...

A week later he wrote again:

I apologize for these poor words. This may become the most unclever love letter written in English. Please try to feel the spirit and do not weigh the words... In your nearness I feel changed. In my eyes you are too good to play a game of love with.

Yours, Walter

Lichtenberg • Trobisch Austrian Home

F I V E

LICHTENBERG 1950

*"It is the heart always
that sees before the head can see."
~Thomas Carlyle~*

We walked and hiked the wooded paths together as if there were no tomorrow. Walter had wanted to show me his favorite place on earth, the Lichtenberg, a mountain firmly bedded in the Upper Austrian foothills of the Alps. Some years from now, our present surroundings would become famous through Julie Andrews' jubilant burst of song on a rounded mountaintop just a few miles to the west. This was *The Sound of Music* country. Our footsteps crunched down on prickly cones and a thick layer of pine needles. We leisurely followed the steep banks of an old woodcutting trail.

How did we end up in this beautiful place?

By June 1950, I had finished my studies in Paris and made preparations for the voyage by ship to West Africa. Before leaving Europe, I accepted Walter's invitation to spend some quiet weeks in Germany with his mother. Her name was Gertrude, just like my mother's. She had been a teacher before her marriage and was a courageous, beautiful woman—a joy-giver with her sharp wit and ability to celebrate.

Then Walter suggested out of the blue that we spend the last days of our vacation with a farmer's family on the

Lichtenberg. The hamlet consisted of five houses, peacefully perched in the middle of a clearing on the mountaintop. To this day, the number of houses has grown from only five to seven! Here Walter had recuperated from his wounds during the war, and the place had grown close to his heart.

I immediately understood why he had to bring me here. How I longed to show him the natural charm of my own Ozark home! For those in love, beauty must be shared.

We had again mounted his famous motorcycle, given to him as a parting gift by the Lutheran youth in America. He praised my growing skills at hanging on and taking the curves with just the right amount of ease. I won't ever forget the breathtaking and exhilarating views of my first trip through the Alps.

"Ingrid, these are the most beautiful places I know," he told me. "The high mountains have been like sermons to me, sermons of the eternal and unchangeable." He made me feel like the wealthiest woman on earth. It was bliss to stand next to the man I loved while we drank in the eternal splendor of the scenic valleys below. I stifled an inner voice that was doing its best to constrict my heart and remind me by the minute that soon we would be separated by continents.

No, there he still was, walking in front of me in a soft flannel shirt, mended at the elbows, slightly frayed at the cuffs. Neither of us had much disposable income, nor did we consider it a high priority to replace worn, but still usable items of clothing. I soon learned that Walter lived in happy oblivion to such matters. He was always more aware of others' soul-needs than of his own wardrobe needs. Again my heart constricted at the thought of having to leave in just a few more days.

Slowly and haltingly Walter began to tell me of his war years.

"I was drafted at the age of 18 and became an infantry soldier in Hitler's army just two weeks after passing my final exams at the Petrusgymnasium in Leipzig. After basic training I was sent to the Russian battlefront. The horrific battle of

Stalingrad became my introduction to the realities of war. We feared freezing to death more than being hit by a deadly bullet. At least the bullet did its job quickly and often mercifully."

"Walter, how can you talk that way?" I protested.

"Dear heart, you have asked me to tell you of the war. Every sentence is a struggle for me. It is easier not to speak than to try to put into words what I lived through. Please try not to question me," he implored. I kept my promise, and only once more in my life did I ask him to tell the story of his war years. It was on a camping trip through southern Europe when our children were teenagers. They needed to know.

"In the winter of 1942 in Stalingrad I could have died a thousand times. What kept me alive were several poems I had written as a Christmas gift to my mother. I kept them hidden in the inner pocket of my uniform. 'I cannot die yet,' I penciled in my journal, 'not until I have posted these.'

"A few days later the military doctor told us men in the foxholes that we had only 24 hours to live. We would either freeze to death or be overrun by the Russian tanks. I volunteered to keep a small fire going through the night in order to melt snow, so that the soldiers would have something warm to drink in the morning. This meant I was in even greater danger of being hit," Walter labored at telling me what happened next.

"You cannot imagine the morning, dear Ingrid. We knew this would be our last day. The first light of dawn brought nothing but beauty and peace and comfort. This unreal sense of floating above the gruesome battle scene spread its wings inside me. One of my friends experienced the very same thing. The more the light of day revealed our hopeless situation, the less our fear controlled us. I opened my devotional booklet (1942 Daily Texts) and read verse 2 from Psalm 18 aloud to every one who could hear: 'THE LORD IS MY SHIELD!'

"At that moment I was shot in the upper leg. Propelled by a strength that was not my own, I crept through the gauntlet of the sniper's fire with bullets whizzing around me for several hundred yards. Again and again I repeated those words, 'The Lord is my shield.' It probably saved me that I couldn't walk or run upright anymore. Next thing I knew, some medics were dragging me to safety. They bound up my wound and threw me in the back of a German Red Cross truck that escaped through a gap in the Russian circle of soldiers surrounding the defeated German army at Stalingrad." It was one of the last vehicles to get out before the Russian ring closed.

Our path had now come to a light-filled clearing in the woods. Bushy, knee-high grass covered the level ground like an unkempt carpet. A warm breeze ruffled the grass as much as it played with our hair. We became a living part of the magical, yet natural setting, resting side by side on a tree stump that dominated our quiet oasis like a throne.

Walter put his arm around me. What he said next was of the utmost importance to him: "It was then, in the turmoil of the Battle of Stalingrad, with only hours to live, that I made a clear decision for Christ. When I was rescued as one of the last survivors, I felt God had laid His hand on me in a special way. From then on I wanted to serve Him and Him alone."

Awestruck, I realized that the miracle of his rescue and his intense conversion had taken place the same year I announced with a trembling voice at my father's memorial service: "My sisters and I are now more determined than ever that we want to give our lives entirely to the expansion of God's kingdom here on earth, in the manner and place which to Him seems best." Remembering again my father's advice, I had prayed with new fervor and urgency for the protection of my future life partner. Many of my classmates and my two older brothers were being trained for active duty after Pearl Harbor. I recall distinctly during this time praying for my partner and having a vision of him lying wounded in the snow. Of course, I never thought he might be a German in Russia. When I shared this with Walter, he held me even closer and kissed me without words.

Enough war talk for one day.

He continued his account on the next day's hike. I was careful not to interrupt.

"After my recovery I was sent back to the front a second time, this time to the Ukraine in Southern Russia. Needless to say, Hitler's war seemed futile and useless to me quite from the beginning. My mother loved to say with her wry and contagious sense of humor, 'From the moment Walter was drafted, Germany began to lose the war.' Of course, my experience in Stalingrad had confirmed rather than changed my opinion of Germany's war effort. You must also remember that at this point my comrades and I were quite unaware of what was happening to our Jewish friends and neighbors back home.

"I recall writing in my journal repeatedly about physically experiencing the nearness of Christ. He walked beside me, clearly and earnestly. He was in me. He walked ahead of me. Yes, He even protected me from behind. The only place I could try to sleep was in a foxhole. My frame of mind did strange things to me. On the one hand I wanted to hang on to my life with every part of my being. On the other hand I rejoiced over the prospect of soon going to heaven."

"God is a verb, not a noun."
~R. Buckminster Fuller~

"The temptation was just to give up and lie down. On September 11, 1943 I read in the Moravian Daily Texts the verse from Isaiah, 'Trust in the Lord forever, for the Lord is an everlasting rock.' Shrapnel hit me on the back of my head and neck. A bullet wounded me in the left arm. I inched my way back, further and further, with great effort and superhuman strength. All the while I was clinging to God as my rock, whether I lived or died. Finally I must have reached a safe place behind the firing lines. Someone bandaged my head to stop the bleeding. My shattered, helpless left arm was bound to my side, and I was placed in a body cast. I was carried to an abandoned hut with dying men all around me. When the medics checked me a few hours later and saw that I still had a pulse, they put me on the last car of the hospital train headed for Vienna, Austria.

"Three days later I was admitted to the Catholic Hospital *Zum Göttlichen Heiland* in that beautiful city."

Little did Walter realize at the time that exactly forty years later his grandson Charles would be born in that very same hospital. Of our fourteen grandchildren, Charles is also the only one to have inherited one of his German grandfather's distinctive features: a dimple on the chin!

As we walked hand in hand, Walter shared with me that there was one art which he had mastered completely—that of being able to fall into a deep sleep the moment his head touched the pillow.

"What's your secret?" I asked.

"All I have to do is think of the sound of those train wheels taking me to Vienna. After the unbelievable trauma of the battlefield, the wheels sang to me: 'You are safe—you are safe—you are safe.'"

That was just an early chapter of his remarkable life journey. Many years later I discovered the letters he had written to his parents during World War II. His mother had carefully sorted them and tied them in neat packets, together with his journals. His younger brother Klaus typed them for me from the old German script. They are a precious treasure and documentation of a story that has not yet been fully told.

My parting from friends in Rock Island had been difficult. My parting from Walter at the Salzburg train station was heartbreaking. Our fatherly friend and counselor, Pastor Fuchs, had told us simply, "A Christian is one who can wait." We knew our friendship was deep and strong and did not doubt it could endure the pain of separation. That assurance, however, did not lessen my very real pain, as I sat on the Mozart Express, inexorably headed back to Paris. No, the wheels were not singing to me, "You are safe. You are safe." Instead they were incessantly hammering in the fact that I was traveling further and further away from my beloved.

In Paris I packed my copper-studded trunk yet another time. I was to sail on the SS Banfora from Marseilles, France, on September 11, 1950. It would take two whole weeks before I reached Douala, Cameroun.

Before Walter left the Lichtenberg in Austria, he wrote to my mother in Bolivia on August 23, 1950:

Dear Mrs. Hult,

Ingrid will have told you about me, so it will not be necessary to introduce myself.

Your daughter has moved many hearts during her stay in Germany. People like her and listen to her message. It is my greatest joy and personal blessing to translate her words. I can really say that we slowly came to know each other through this teamwork for the Gospel. From the very beginning, the basis of our relationship was not emotional. We were simply brought together for common service.

Neither of us has forced anything. How can we, having such different plans and calls for the future? I never would dare to step into Ingrid's life out of a self-made decision. But the less we do, the more the Lord does.

Here on this mountain farm, two hours by foot from the next village, we had time to be quiet together. We read the Bible and prayed. There is great harmony, but also great calmness between us. Humanly speaking, the future seems foggy. Under the light of God's Word and in the atmosphere of His fellowship, everything is clear.

We have no doubts in our heart that Ingrid has to go to Africa. Just this risk on God, this insecurity, this not knowing what the Lord is going to do, is a spiritual adventure that allures us and strengthens our faith.

Last night Ingrid told the farmers and their families here on the Lichtenberg the story of your family. Looking upon all these merciful actions of the Lord, how can we ever be afraid of anything?

May the Lord bless you and your work! Thank you for your prayers.

Yours in Christ Jesus,
Walter

Seven years later to the day that Walter was wounded in the Ukraine and was able to crawl to safety because of God's promise to him, I boarded the ship that was to take me to Africa. Here are excerpts from my weekly letters to Walter as I embarked on that great adventure.

On board the SS Banfora, September 11, 1950
Dear Walter,

Our ship just slipped gracefully out of the ancient harbor of Marseilles into the calm waters of the Mediterranean. The weather is perfect. I found a quiet spot on deck, hidden behind a pile of ropes, where I can watch the sea and write to you.

'I love you, Lord God, and you make me strong.' The first verse from Psalm 18, is my promise of the day. I need it, for I am very lonesome. I'm the only American on board. Most of the other passengers on this French ship are colonial government administrators who, with their wives and children, are on their way to a post in French West Africa. They seem to celebrate a lot, making the most of their last fourteen days in a cultured setting.

Dakar, September 18, 1950
Dear Walter,

We have just pulled into the harbor of Dakar. You can see it on your map right on the big hump of Africa. I just found this entry in my father's journal. After fifteen days at sea when he caught his first glimpse of Africa, he wrote:

'I was up long before dawn as our ship prepared to dock in Dakar. I could see the light of land blinking in the darkness. Then the black outline of earth meeting sea. In a moment it was gray—not gradu-

ally, but suddenly. I thought, nothing stops this advance of light once the dawn begins—just as if a curtain had been raised…'

Now it is thirty years later. My first impression—the fine hands of the African porters who have come on board to help unload baggage.

Walter, sometimes my life is so full of new impressions that I fear I cannot do them justice. It is so good to know that you are listening. I just walked for the first time on African soil. What beautiful colors—the dark green palms contrasting with the brown tile roofs, cream-colored buildings and almost red earth. As for the Africans, I observed a kind of resignation—no complaining or desperation—just a quiet acceptance of their lot in life.

As for the two of us, I wouldn't want it any other way. There's a delightful uncertainty about the future. God has certainly used unique methods to bring us together. The work that we both have to do will give meaning to our separation. I agree with your words in your last letter: 'Let's both work as if there would be no love, and love as if there would be no work.'

At sea, September 23, 1950

Dear Walter,

This is my last night at sea. Tomorrow we shall be in Douala! My heart is filled with mingled emotions—to think that I am now so close to the land to which God has called me.

Last night I dreamed of my father. He was so very real. You were there too, and we all three talked together. Even after I woke up, his presence lingered, so that it was hard to persuade myself that it had been a dream.

Douala, September 25, 1950

Dear Walter,

After we sailed past the majestic Mount Cameroun bathed in glorious afternoon sunlight, we anchored in Douala harbor at four o'clock. A crowd of people waited at the pier. I did not expect anyone to meet me because our closest mission station is a thousand miles inland. But then I heard someone calling my name. It was Mr. Monnier, a French-speaking Swiss, who meets arriving missionaries.

In a few minutes he had my baggage off the boat and was escorting me to my room in the old mission house.

After I was settled, he excused himself, because he and his wife had a dinner invitation. I smiled bravely, finding myself all alone in a gray, uninviting room with the African night coming on. From without I heard the street cries and was overwhelmed by a heavy sense of loneliness. I tried hard not to feel afraid and walked up and down the old wooden verandah, listening to all the strange new sounds.

"Nothing in life is to be feared.
It is only to be understood."
~Marie Currie~

But then as I walked, I knew I was not alone. I could feel His very presence and the heavy weight lifted from my heart.

What joy to get your first letter that had come to Mr. Monnier's office! You wrote:

Ludwigshaven, October 8, 1950
Dear Jungle Queen,
It's been a great adventure to be with you, dear Ingrid, but it will be a still greater adventure of obedience to let you go and walk with you through this hard school of believing without seeing.
Faith is a risk on God. Life is a risk on God. It all will make sense one day. Nothing will be in vain. He will illuminate our darkness in His time. Our separation will become a great finding-again, more beautiful than ever. We are living through a time of certain uncertainty, a kind of blind flight in a definite direction.
Your German Prince

Walter's words comforted me over and over again. For the first time, I became aware of his unique gift to express the simplest and most profound truths in clear, articulate, yet beautiful language. His comforting love reached out to me and held me safe.

Douala, October 15, 1950

Dear Walter-Prince,

It is raining—as it has done almost every hour since my arrival. Douala is the second rainiest city in the world, and this is the height of the rainy season. A tropical downpour is no gentle pitter-patter, but an unremitting deluge in sheets. When the rain stops, it is steamy. The atmosphere is like being in a hot house. The sheets on my bed are always clammy. Mold gathers on my shoes. Everything has a musty, tropical smell.

Just when my spirits hit rock bottom, I received word from Mr. Okland, one of our missionaries who is supposed to meet me in Yaounde, the capital of Cameroun, that because of the heavy rains he won't be able to get through until the end of October.

And so I wait—for the ship from America, which is to bring my baggage, and for the railroad to be repaired after another landslide. Mr. Monnier likes to tease me. 'Hurry up and get ready, Ingrid,' he says, 'Your train is leaving next month.' I guess Pastor Fuchs is right. A Christian is one who can wait.

This week began with a wonderful promise: 'I ... will make you prosper more than before. Then you will know that I am the Lord' (Ezekiel 36:11). I am learning to walk through the fog, or here you might say rain, with the hope of a promise in my heart.

"The end of a matter is better than its beginning,
and patience is better than pride."
~Ecclesiastes 7:8~

Douala, October 20, 1950

Dear Walter,

I'm typing out a large packet of notes written by my father as he was exploring the territory in northern Cameroun and Chad thirty years ago. Suddenly I came across an entry written by my mother in 1923, describing their stay in Douala at the old Basel Mission House. This is the very place where I'm staying. It changes my perspective completely. I'm starting to feel at home.

Yaounde, October 28, 1950
Dear Walter,

Movement at last. The train is rolling and climbing steadily toward the capital through some of the densest vegetation I have ever seen. I begin to understand what a bush knife is needed for... Africa is like an inverted saucer. The low-altitude coastal areas form a rim while the higher plateaus dominate the center.

Garoua-Boulai, November 6, 1950
Dear Walter,

Greetings from our first station! Every bone and muscle seems sore from bouncing in a Dodge pickup truck over unbelievably bumpy and muddy roads. Sometimes I looked twice trying to determine whether the road was still what I might call a road or just some mucky cow tracks. But no, on we went, finally coming to a little sign signaling the proximity of a Mission Protestante. Looking up the hill, I saw two simple missionary homes and a cluster of native huts. A minute later our truck was surrounded by the children of missionaries who attend school here. 'Welcome to our family—Psalm 67' was on my place card at the gala dinner that evening.

On Sunday I gave my first greeting to African Christians in the little grass-roofed chapel, filled to over-flowing. I told them about my father, Ralph Hult, who had come thirty years earlier and had always wanted to come back. I told them how happy I was that I could help his life's dream come true and that in my heart I already felt like I had been here many times before.

How could I know then that my daughter Ruth would be born here a decade later? And that she would come to this very place to serve as a medical student for one summer...

Poli. November 16, 1950

Dear Walter,

Another two days of hard travel. Gone is the exotic tropical beauty of the coast. I left Marseilles well over two months ago! We just crossed a magnificent mountain range. Then the Benoue River. Since it's dry season, a heavy woven straw mat is placed across the dry riverbed just like a carpet. We drove on it feeling like royalty. The Africans around our Poli station danced for joy when we pulled up. Everything inside me felt like dancing too. What a trip!

The first to greet me was Samuel, belonging to the Sara tribe, the people to whom my father had felt drawn. He kept saying "Sanoo! Sanoo!" which in Fulani is both a greeting and an expression of thankfulness for our safe arrival. Harriet, who had been a fellow student with me in Paris, came running. It was so good to see a familiar face. We will be working together here.

Slowly I learn to keep house African-style. Water must be carried up from the river, boiled and filtered, before we can use it. Wood is our fuel, but our helper must go a couple of miles into the forest to fetch it, carrying it back to our hut on his head. Kerosene lamps must be cleaned and filled, mosquito nets put up, in addition to dozens of other duties not needed back home.

Poli, March 6, 1951

Dear Walter,

One writer called Africa the continent of God's adventure waiting for God's adventurers. Poli is beautifully situated in the highlands, but also quite hot. It is right in the center of a great Muslim territory, unoccupied by any colonial power. The needs I see around me are endless. Superstition, fear, and poverty enslave the people. They lack medical supplies and treatment for even the most basic of injuries.

My duties, adventures, and lessons learned could fill yet another book. The letters between Germany and Cameroun continued to flow. About a year into my term, I fell desperately ill. We had no doctor, so I was loaded into our *missionary ambulance*, a maroon-colored Chevy delivery truck with Beryl Sand as my nurse. As I lay on the kapok mattress in the bed of the truck, drifting in and out of consciousness, I kept saying the words, "I cannot die yet," just as Walter had said them when he faced death in the cold of the Russian winter. We finally reached Ngaoundere where the Norwegian doctor diagnosed severe hepatitis. It took weeks to recover.

That September I moved 350 miles south from Poli to Garoua-Boulai to teach the children of our missionaries. It had a better climate and was more centrally located. I carried the responsibility of teaching thirteen eager children ranging from second-graders to first-year high school students. I taught more than thirty courses a day, carefully prepared and outlined by the Calvert School in Maryland. Classes began at eight a.m. and ended at five p.m.

Walter and I continued to search for guidance for our future. I asked him in a letter, "Would you come to Africa if I were not here?" He answered:

> *What a foolish question! You are asking a question which even God doesn't ask. Don't you know that you are an important part of the guidance that helps to point me in the right direction? Recently when I talked it over with Pastor Fuchs, he looked at me with his piercing blue eyes and said, 'Walter, the question is not, why go? But, why not go?' Especially now when the Iron Curtain prevents me from returning to my home and ministry in East Germany, I could not find a single good reason for not going to Africa.*

Walter chided me, "Maybe you have a 'call cramp.' You want to dictate to God how the call should come."

It was then, after we had been separated for almost a year, that he opened his heart to me:

> *My Dearest,*
>
> *For a young woman, the power of sexuality sleeps until it is awakened by words and gestures. The hedge of thorns in the story of Sleeping Beauty is a picture of this protection. I would have been irresponsible to start this fire in your heart unless I was ready to share my whole life with you. That is why I was careful up till now not to write passionate love letters. It was just because I loved you that I held back. But now it is different and I can tell you the hour has come...*

Will you be my wife? ... I know, too, I must win you anew every day. Forgive my awkwardness and clumsiness.
In deep love,
Your Walter

I replied from Garoua-Boulai that same month, September 1951:

My darling Walter,
  If I say, 'Yes, I will marry you,' does that mean we are engaged in God's sight? If so, then we can share the most secret things in our hearts. Don't you have any fear about the risk you are taking? I do.
  In the story of Sleeping Beauty, I'm wondering what the Prince did after he woke her up. Don't you think he was very careful, so she wouldn't be afraid? Then he told her of his love. He was surely kind and thoughtful and won her heart. Their love could then grow from a small bud to a full blossoming flower.
  When I think of being a partner with you in God's kingdom, there is great joy in my heart. Because I believe too, that love is a risk on God, I dare to answer your question with a glad, 'Yes, I will become your wife.'
  Your Jungle Queen

We agreed that we would be engaged by long distance on October 14, 1951—Walter in Europe and I in Africa. Thirty years earlier Walter's parents had become engaged on this day. It was also his father's 63rd birthday. We would not announce our engagement though until Christmas. I spent the evening of our special day walking alone under a full moon in an African orange grove. The trees were in full blossom and the fragrant scent of the beautiful white flowers filled my soul with longing. I tried hard to remember what it had felt like when we sat on the tree stump in Austria together, and he had gently put his arm around me.

Walter's letters were filled with the romance of courtship as well as the steady growth of commitment and love. On December 30, 1951 he wrote from Ludwigshafen:

My Beloved,

I wait—like a tree—its branches stretched toward heaven. Everything is frozen, everything is sleeping and everything waits to be awakened through the warmth of your presence. It is like entering a sanctuary. This deep secret encompasses me: Here is a person who wants to give herself to me—body and soul—completely... A thousand times I have tried to imagine the moment when we will see each other. How often I hold conversations with you; thinking out the answers you would give and knowing your answers are going to be even more beautiful.

I call out to you ever louder across the wide oceans and continents, 'Come here.'...

We set the date and place of our wedding, June 2, 1952, in Mannheim, Germany. I spent happy hours designing and sewing my wedding dress on the little Singer, cranking it with my right hand while I guided the seam with my left. I finished the school year, and after a happy farewell from students and co-workers, I set off on the greatest adventure of my life—to become the wife of Walter Trobisch.

Walter and Ingrid on their honeymoon

S I X

BUILDING BRIDGES

"With joy you will draw water from the wells of salvation."
~Isaiah 12:3~

When I announced my engagement at Christmas time to my fellow missionaries, they agreed unanimously that I be granted a leave of absence upon completion of the school year. However, our mission board in Minneapolis asked me to postpone our wedding. I did not consider that for a moment.

On May 11, 1952 I boarded the Air France flight from Fort Lamy, Chad to Paris, France. After my two years in the tropics it was a culture shock to sit in this elegant, air-conditioned plane. As we flew over the Sahara desert in the moonlight, I tried to feel my feelings. I had no great sense of elation or of overwhelming joy. I had made a conscious decision—one that would affect my whole life. There was no turning back.

The image of building bridges between three continents spoke to my heart. It also helped me face some of my fears about marrying into a new world and a new way of thinking. All I knew for sure was that I was going in the right direction.

Theo Bovet, our counselor and trusted friend, had written us from his home in Switzerland: "First you choose the one you love, and then you love the one you've chosen." At this point, the first step, the choosing step, seemed the easier part. But what about loving the one whom I barely knew for the rest of my life?

I was afraid of my own courage. This man that I was to marry in a few days spoke a different language. He had a different heritage. He had fought on one side in World War II. My two older brothers were on the other side: Paul in the Marine Air Force in the Pacific and John who was now serving as a doctor to the U.S. Armed Forces in Germany. How did this all fit together?

Friends in Paris handed me a letter that Walter had sent to them. "Not to be opened until you are on the train to Germany," he had written on the sealed blue envelope in his bold, even script.

The second-class compartment was empty on that splendid morning in May, and the vivid images outside my train window remain with me to this day. Bombed out buildings and ruined bridges, the scars of war, were softened by the radiant beauty of spring as the train headed closer and closer toward the French-German border. I closed my eyes and quietly prayed for a calm spirit, before carefully opening the envelope and unfolding Walter's letter:

Dear Ingrid,

In a few hours you will meet that person with whom you will share your life. What he is and how he is—that will be decisive for your whole life…

He is a person—not a god. He has many faults and weaknesses and is in constant battle with himself. He does not want to be idolized by you. He only wants to be as he is—and as he is—he wants to be loved by you.

The person that you will be meeting is a man. This means that at least in the beginning he will hide his deepest feelings because he believes it is unmanly to reveal them. At the same time, his heart is overcome by the greatness of this moment. That's why he will act as if it's something that happens every day. In the first minutes of the en-

counter he will probably flee into conversation about the practical things close at hand, and he will be happy that they are there. He will try to hide his deep inner feelings and will be proud of himself if he succeeds. That's how foolish a man is. That is why you shouldn't be fooled by him. How he really is—that's up to you to perceive and to ascertain.

But he will not always be like this. He just wants to bridge over those first moments of embarrassment and take you to a lonely place where he has you all to himself and where he can reveal his true feelings to you.

He has never opened up to another person as he has opened up to you. That is why he is also trembling as he thinks of the encounter with you. For he knows that you shall be that person whom he will allow to see through him, just as he allows God to see through him. In the trembling though, there is a holy joy—joy that such a person exists.

He loves you. He has made up his mind to say yes to you as you are. It is easy for him to say this yes because he knows that he can say it to no other person.

He loves you. He is ready to give himself up to you, and he knows that he will come out of the encounter a different man than he was before...

He loves you. He wants to be able to give you all that he has. God has given him many things. He is very happy when he can also give it to you...

The train will only stop a few more times, and then he will stand before you. You must be very calm and composed. The greatest hours of God in our lives are the more powerful if we keep a calm and quiet heart.

Yours,
Walter

He waited on the platform, red roses in his hand. When his arms enfolded me, I knew I had come home. We had two weeks to prepare for our wedding.

Germany requires a civil wedding ceremony for legal marriage. It had taken months to get the papers necessary for our marriage license. Walter wrote in our new joint journal, a small loose-leaf binder:

Here I am once more at the Standesamt, the German legal office we must deal with. This has taken a lot of time, a lot of papers, and a lot of money. Every official paper Ingrid sent me from Africa had to have two translations because she was in a French-speaking territory and because the papers were in English.

And the questions they asked me:

'Where was your fiancée born?'—'In Tanzania.'
'Which part of Germany is that?'—'It's in Africa.'
'Is she an African?'—'No, she's an American.'
'Of what descent?'—'Swedish.'
'Where does her mother live?'—'In Bolivia, South America.'
'What's her name?'—'Gertrude L. Hult.'
'What does the L. Stand for?'—'I don't know.'

Then you can't get your marriage license until you find out. In Germany no initial letters are permitted.'

June 2, 1952. Here I stood, legally married at last, hugging my dear mother, outside the beautiful Christuskirche in Mannheim, one of the few churches in that city not damaged by bombs. Mother had finished her term in Bolivia, and with help from friends and family, she was able to come to our wedding. I had not seen my mother for seven years!

German handshakes are no laughing matter. I learned that as Walter and I stood in the open church portal, receiving the well wishes of everyone. He had invited members of his former congregation, and every single one showed up—at least that is what I was beginning to think. The stream of oncoming people did not want to end.

"Walter, now they all know who I am," I told my handsome groom rather helplessly, "but I feel like I don't know a single one of your friends."

I felt alone because none of my siblings had been able to come.

"Ouch," I exclaimed under my breath while politely enduring yet another one of those more than firm handshakes, accompanied by a beaming face. In the tradition of the land we had decided to wear our new wedding rings on our right hand, instead of the left as we do in the States.

Walter introduced the next young lady in line as Anneliese Willin, a faithful member of his youth group. Anneliese, in her excitement, simply didn't stop pumping my hand. By now, I was sure, painful blisters were beginning to form around my treasured new wedding ring. I wondered if the same thing had happened to Walter.

We had chosen simple golden bands. Our wedding date, June 2, 1952, had been engraved on the inside along with the verse from Isaiah that we had chosen as our life motto together. (My parents had done the same thing with Psalm 67:1,2 as their life prayer.)

During a moment's delay in the receiving line I quietly showed Walter the inside of my hand. He laughed as he opened up his hand to show me his very own red marks of torture. (The next day we did switch our rings to the left hand!)

"With joy we are drawing water and blisters from the wells of salvation, dear Ingrid. Next time we might be drawing coffee-colored water from a river in Africa, but whatever we draw, let's always do it with joy and together!" Then the next wedding guest called for his attention.

My pain subsided into something very close to bliss. This was the day we had both been longing for after nearly two years of separation.

A June breeze picked up my bridal veil and blew it across Walter's face. He barely noticed because he was listening so intently to the elderly man next in line. I could tell this man was unburdening his soul to Walter, right there on the church steps on our wedding day. Suddenly it was I who had become the observer and outsider. With a pang I realized that this probably would not be the only time when I was to share the attention of my concerned and caring husband with someone who needed him even more than I did. In our many years of married life I always struggled with these unexpected and intrusive demands on Walter's time.

Germans do know how to celebrate! The afternoon's festivities quickly dispelled my shadowy thoughts. This day of joy was a precious gift. Everyone present had suffered through the horrors of war, and the experience had intensified their ability to *seize the moment by its collar*, a wonderful German saying, and immortalize the occasion with verse and song.

Pastor Fuchs was a very able master of ceremonies as Walter's friends and parents shared toasts and memories. His mother had managed to slip across the East German border a few days earlier. She had written a table song in German, French, and English relating the whole story of the Hult-Trobisch romance. She invited all the guests to join in the refrain. The merriment in that festively decorated hall was downright contagious. Our program lasted over three hours. Walter's father shared a moving toast. It had been more difficult for him to get a pass from the authorities in East Germany to attend his son's wedding than for me to come from another continent.

We celebrated on that day the completion of a human bridge, planned, built, and joined together by God. We came from two nations, two families, and two sexes. Walter had grown up in Leipzig, a large city in Saxony, Germany. I had grown up in the Midwest of the United States. I was 26 years old. He was 28. We each had a strong home base—good parents, siblings, lots of peers, but most important of all was that we shared a common faith. We realized how vital this foundation would be for overcoming the difficulties that were bound to arise in our cross-cultural marriage.

During our very first breakfast together we read the scripture verses for June 3rd, 1952 in the Moravian Daily Texts. From then on, we began every day in the same way. We celebrated the gift of the new morning by becoming quiet together. It became a habit and a way of focusing our hearts on God and on each other's needs. Notebooks in hand, we individually wrote our answers to the following questions, an inner discipline Walter had learned from Martin Luther's example and applied to his own life:

What am I thankful for?
What am I sorry about?
What should I ask for?
What shall I do?

The Scripture verses would guide us in articulating our answers. Then we shared our written insights. By writing things down, our dialogue with God and with each other became tangible and visible and concrete. We had written proof of the goals we set. We became accountable to each other for what had convicted us and for the ways we wanted to change.

"The palest ink is stronger than the best memory."
~Chinese Proverb~

I won't forget the first time we had the following interaction:

"Ingrid, I think you wrote too many items under question number 4, the 'what shall I do today' question," Walter told me point blank. "Perhaps you need to go back and have a second quiet time and take off that list anything God doesn't want you to do today."

When he told me this for the first time, I was actually quite furious. Who was he to determine whether my list was too long or not?

"I'm in a hurry, Walter. Let's just get on with our day. I promise to write a shorter list tomorrow."

"Darling, that's exactly the problem," he replied with an undertone of impatience. "God gave us 24 hours in a day and in His wisdom certainly supplied ample time to accomplish what He wants us to accomplish. You put yourself and me, your dear husband, under stress if you overburden yourself with more duties than you have time for. And by the way, have you thought to include your own needs anywhere on your list? I'm not interested in an angelic, but exhausted wife."

He needed to explain no more. I understood the deep love that motivated his request. It was surprisingly easy to cross off a few items and streamline my goals. From then on he only had to remind me once of my need for a second quiet time, and I would obediently comply. In his love he helped me to set boundaries and to say no when necessary—one of the hardest things for me to learn in life.

*"Neither natural love nor divine love will remain
unless it is cultivated.
We must form the habit of love
until it is the practice in our lives."
~Oswald Chambers~*

Our quiet time always ended with prayer. It took a little while to be entirely comfortable together while talking out loud to God. We smilingly assured ourselves that God could certainly understand German as well as English as well as any mixture of the two, however the words tumbled out. And it was also okay to be silent and just to listen. Prayer surely entailed more than a one-way monologue directed towards God.

Walter and I found that writing down what we had heard was also a great help for decision-making. We were often asked in later years by our friends, "What's your secret? How do you manage to get so many things done and still have time for people?" I liked to tell them that I had "gotten my commands straight" while being quiet in the morning. Walter would quote George MacDonald's words: "I work under God's orders, but not under my own steam." We also determined that people should come before programs.

On our honeymoon we visited friends in France, Switzerland, and Germany. Travel by motorcycle was cheap. We packed our small wardrobe into a much-used canvas fold-up suitcase and belted it securely on the baggage carrier behind my seat. Then, with a thermos of hot coffee and lunch in the saddlebags, we set out.

We had little money, but lots of time. Neither of us had a salaried job, Walter having resigned as youth pastor and I on leave of absence from the mission field in Cameroun. There was a new mission board now responsible for the Sudan Mission. Walter had sent in his official application to them. Would they be willing to accept him without a personal interview? We were living in Germany, and the board was in the U.S. Would Walter, as a German, ever be granted a visa to enter French territory—especially in Cameroun—where no Germans had been allowed to live since World War I?

In the meantime we accepted invitations to speak together about God's unusual guidance in our lives. I remember the time Walter was asked to prepare a sermon on the text from Galatians 6:2: "Bear one another's burdens, and so fulfill the law of Christ." He entitled his sermon *Sharing*.

Someone had given us a perfectly shaped red apple almost twice the size of a normal apple, juicy, the only one from a young tree. On Sunday morning I polished the marvelous piece of fruit, cut it into eight perfect slices and arranged them with great care on a plate that I set on Walter's desk. As he reached for the first slice, he told me that in his sermon he would talk about sharing as a way of multiplying our joys and dividing our sorrows. He then happily devoured the second slice as we began our quiet time and morning devotions together, and so I watched the apple disappear, slice by slice. He continued to go on about the virtues of sharing, his mind and spirit totally absorbed by the morning's sermon topic.

When the apple was gone, and I had not had a single bite, my tears burst forth.

"How could you be so thoughtless and eat that entire apple while talking all the time about sharing?" The vehemence of my accusations and hurt feelings even caught me by surprise.

He looked at me quite puzzled, and with amazement he realized what he had done.

"Forgive me, Ingrid. My thoughts weren't on the apple. I did not consciously eat it. As a matter of fact, I don't think I even tasted it. Please forgive me. I was selfish and unthinking." He reached for my hand and tried to comfort me.

He did try hard to be more thoughtful after that, but I also learned two valuable lessons as a young wife. My new husband was single-minded about his purpose in preparing and proclaiming Christ's message. That could also make him very absentminded regarding other things, let alone something as inconsequential as an apple, as beautiful and special as it may have been. I had to learn to love and accept him as he was, even with his unique brand of inattentiveness.

The second thing I learned, and that I have shared with young wives ever since, is that only a baby has the right to be understood without words, but not a grown woman. Why did I have to watch him quietly as he devoured that apple and then, after the fact, loudly accuse him of not being sensitive to my feelings? Many partners can fall into the trap of thinking that, if our spouse truly loves us, he should intuitively know how and what we are feeling. How can he if we don't tell him?

Communication is hard work. It is like building a bridge between two people, stone by stone, over many years.

When our marriage was only a few months old, we had to make a life decision. Two letters reached us on the same day in Ludwigshafen in our cozy one room apartment. One was a call to be directors of a planned Retreat Center in southern Germany. The other was a letter of call to Walter from the

American Lutheran Church to our mission field in Cameroun.

We sat down together and prayed that God would guide us. We discussed both calls. Either one could be God's will for our lives. Then with our notebooks in hand, we listened intently to what we felt God was saying to us. Each of us wrote down the pros and cons. We then read to each other what we had written. To both of us it had become clear that God was pointing us to Africa.

---

*"Prayer is a heart-to-heart conversation with God
who we know loves us."*
~*St. Teresa of Avila*~

Our mission board then sent us to Paris where Walter and I studied at the Paris Mission School of Theology for several months. On a Sunday morning in May 1953, after packing ten pieces of baggage and sending it by freight to our ship, we got on our trusty Horex, made three rounds encircling the Arch of Triumph, and headed for Bordeaux. Four days later we boarded the SS General LeClerq for Africa. Our time on this French ship was like the honeymoon we never had. After a voyage of two weeks we landed in Douala, Cameroun. It was our first wedding anniversary.

We stayed at the same gray, wooden guesthouse where I had spent a month three years before. I remembered the loneliness and fear of my first night on African soil. Walter leaned beside me over the railing of the same wooden verandah where I had paced up and down. Our eyes gazed at the setting sun and watched it drop below the horizon in just a few minutes. He watched in amazement as I explained to him how our nearness to the equator affected the speed of the sunset so there was no twilight. Darkness enfolded us.

"We are where we are meant to be, Ingrid." Walter took me in his arms and kissed me ever so gently on the cheek. "I love you."

Our mission sent us to Tchollire in the territory of Rey Bouba, a semi-autonomous Kingdom in northern Cameroun. King Rey Bouba welcomed us when he heard that my father had visited his father 30 years earlier. We found ourselves in the midst of a vast Muslim territory. We found our best approach was to minister to the sick. We spent our mornings taking care of the 30-40 patients in front of our dispensary door. In the afternoons we taught literacy classes, using simple Bible stories which he had translated into the Fulani language. We watched light come into darkness as they began to understand God's message of love.

After three years the first seven Christians were ready to be baptized. Among these was the first Christian couple. We realized that we could proclaim the gospel effectively only if we had a message on family life. For years missionaries had been preaching to converts, "Do not commit adultery." But no one had taught them the basic concept of a monogamous Christian marriage: How does one man live in harmony and peace with one woman? King Rey Bouba himself had a harem of fifty wives!

Often in those newlywed days we would sit in front of the straw-covered little mud hut we called home. When it got dark, observing the immense star-studded African sky became one of our treasured diversions.

By necessity we had to become our own best source of entertainment. Walter's indomitable sense of humor kept me smiling again and again. He even numbered our favorite jokes so that all he had to announce in his best preacher's voice was, "Number 156, darling!" and we would both succumb to mirthful peels of laughter.

This was only one of the many ways our wedding promise began to fulfill itself. We certainly drew much joyful water from the wells of salvation. With no distractions and plenty of frustration and hardship around us, we had to appeal right to the source of our faith and our strength. I thanked God many times for Walter's incredible gift to make others (and himself!) laugh. In fact, if he could not laugh, things were serious indeed.

After four years in the pioneer outpost of Tchollire on a high arid plateau, Walter was asked to be professor of German and chaplain at Cameroun Christian College in Libamba, located in the midst of the dense rain forest. We spent six years there in what our French colleagues called *the green prison*. It was like living in a greenhouse with 100% humidity. Mold would grow on our leather shoes overnight. Pillows always smelled musty. Our home was made out of prefabricated metal hospital units and stood on stilts.

Our 300 students came from 30 different tribes, the cream of the crop of French-speaking West Africa. Many students attended at great sacrifice to their families. All of the education was done in French, using the same curriculum and textbooks as in France. The faculty was made up of Europeans, Americans, and Africans. Each teacher was paid by the church that had sent her or him. The college was a joint project of several mission groups. Because of our own international marriage, we were often asked to help bridge cultural and inter-personal gaps.

> *"The man who can make hard things easy is the educator."*
> ~Ralph Waldo Emerson~

"If you want to learn about a subject, just teach it," Walter always said. As a chaplain, he also found himself frequently overwhelmed by the personal counseling needs of his students and sometimes even of his colleagues. He began to receive letters from young Africans asking such questions as, "What is most important—sex, love, or marriage? Which one comes first in a relationship?" They trusted him with their most personal and intimate problems. Together we would sit by the kerosene lamp of our dining table and discuss for hours how these questions might best be addressed. How could we make abstract concepts real and practical?

When he saw the great need, Walter proposed to the faculty that he teach a class on marriage to the older students. Dr. Theo Bovet's book on marriage written in French would be the text. Our African students were eager to learn about the Europeans' secrets in this field.

We studied and searched what the Bible had to say and began to articulate sexual issues in our own words, something neither of us had heard discussed in our theological training.

One definitive verse is repeated four times in Scripture: "For this cause a man shall leave his father and his mother and shall cleave to his wife and they shall become one flesh." (Genesis 2:24) We simplified this message down to:

Leaving father and mother—marriage

Cleaving—love

Becoming one flesh—sex

These three stand for *commitment*, *communication*, and *cohabitation*. Slowly one of our key teachings on marriage was being born. Walter and I prayerfully uncovered the message of healing and hoped that God was bidding us proclaim to others regarding the strong bond of Christian marriage. Walter called it the *dynamic triangle*. We began to define a few key terms that helped us identify marital problems more clearly:

If there was no leaving, no commitment, we talked of the sickness of a stolen marriage.

If there was no love, no communication, Walter called it the empty marriage.

If there was no becoming one flesh, no cohabitation, we spoke about the hungry marriage.

"Life together is like a tree
which must grow out of deep roots,
quietly, hidden, strong and in freedom
with no quick blossoming,
no forced hothouse growth."
~Dietrich Bonhoeffer~

We began to think of our own ten-year-old marriage as a tree which had been planted on the day of our wedding. We needed to nurture and water it carefully if it were to grow up straight and tall, and if its branches were to bear fruit.

Sometimes, at the end of a long and exhausting day, I had to tell Walter, "Our tree desperately needs watering today, dear." This became our cue for a long evening walk, hand in hand, quietly and at peace with each other despite the eerie evening sounds of the African jungle.

Yes, I had come a long way in communicating my own needs since our little apple tragedy. Both of us smiled now when we remembered that fateful Sunday morning.

"I miss the crisp, clear alpine air of the Lichtenberg," Walter told me on one of our evening walks. How well I understood his longing. Breathing in the sultry and humid air of the tropics often felt like breathing in water.

We walked down the road for quite some time without saying much. He was deep in thought.

"Building bridges horizontally between people," he mused out loud, "and vertically between people and God is an awesome responsibility. I remember one of my last assignments as a soldier in Bavaria. We were actually supposed to blow up a bridge, so that the enemy could not advance. My comrades and I carefully placed the dynamite and laid a long fuse. But then, wonder of wonders, nobody in the entire patrol had matches!"

He followed his train of thought with growing excitement, "Ingrid, sometimes we're not just called to help build bridges, but we must also save the ones that are there and in danger of being destroyed by a dying relationship."

"Yes, Walter," I added thoughtfully. "You cannot have good roads without good bridges."

Daniel, Ingrid, David, Ruth, Stephen, Walter
Katrine, David and Christine Stewart

SEVEN

THE GIFT OF LOVE

*"Take good care of the pregnant woman.
She is the most important person in our tribe."*
~Chagga Chief~

August 1955. In two weeks I was to give birth to our first child. Walter and I were in our fourth year of marriage and our joy at becoming parents was great. But first we had to get from our outpost in Tchollire to the Mission Hospital in Ngaoundere in time for the birth. That meant crossing the Benoue River at its highest rainy season level. I sat in the hollowed-out log canoe trying to balance the German wicker basket (Reisekorb) that was to be our baby's first bed. I had carefully lined it with a soft old blanket and a white sheet. The mattress was made of unbleached muslin and then filled with kapok from an African tree with cotton-like seeds. Inside the sturdy basket I had put the two dozen diapers and the cotton shirts ordered months before from Montgomery Ward.

As Walter and I crossed the swollen river, I watched with consternation as the water seeped into the bottom of the canoe and soaked my precious bassinet.

"Walter, I could honestly cry. I do know we'll make it across one way or the other, but I put so much love into preparing that basket for our child..." I tried hard not to voice my inmost longing for a clean, dry, comfortable, safe place for the imminent birth. I missed not having a real home made of stones like in the Ozarks. The thick walls of our home in Tchollire were made of mud and stones. A layered roof of thatched reeds protected us from the rain and the sun. Often the roar of lions would wake us up in the middle of the night. I was homesick for my mother. I wanted my sisters to be close by. My husband, however, seemed far more concerned about bailing the brown river water out of the canoe than about my feelings.

Some words from our quiet time that morning came to my rescue:

"Can God do what He likes in your life?
Can He help Himself liberally to you?"
~Oswald Chambers~

Well, God was painting a picture of what that meant right in front of my eyes. I half smiled. The greedy African river was helping itself liberally to my baby basket, but nothing really would be harmed. I knew, I too was safe, even if my circumstances weren't the way I had imagined them for the arrival of our first child. God was simply helping Himself liberally to my life, and I had given Him the go-ahead a long time ago.

We made it safely across the river where Dr. Eastwold met us in his Landrover. After six more hours of hard and bumpy travel we arrived at the modest new Mission Hospital in Ngaoundere where I would be giving birth.

The next day was a restful Sunday before labor contractions began in earnest late Monday afternoon. I looked again at the Daily Text for August 22, 1955. It was Psalm 34:4: "I sought the Lord. He answered me and delivered me from all my fears." I hung on to that promise and held Walter's hand as labor intensified and the contractions came closer together.

My husband stood faithfully by, until Dr. Eastwold said that it might be an all-night vigil, and counseled him to get a little sleep. The contractions were still several minutes apart.

Between the short waves of pain I heard the even hissing of the gas lamp and relaxed. I looked at our empty basket. With loving care I had washed and dried its contents all over again since our adventurous trip.

"Soon it will no longer be empty," I thought and was strangely comforted.

Alice, the doctor's wife stood by and encouraged me. My hard *travail*, which means *work* in French, did not want to end. But as I ascended the crest of each wave and then took a deep cleansing breath, she told me, "Say good-bye to that contraction. You won't see it again. You're climbing a high mountain. Every step gets you nearer the goal."

Then it all happened at once. There was no let-up for me during this steep transition phase as our baby made its way into the birth canal. My body trembled violently. I could no longer think straight. The doctor took over. "Tell Walter to come quickly," he told his wife. Just in time, Walter was at my side. I was filled with exhilaration and joy when, after three hard pushes, our baby was born, and I heard her first unbelievable cry.

"It's a girl!" Dr. Eastwold announced.

"Thank God," Walter said, "for then she will never have to be a soldier."

When I awoke the next morning, I immediately looked at the basket sitting on a low table at the foot of our bed. Had I dreamed? Was the basket still empty? All was so quiet. Then I heard little sounds coming from within the depths of the softly lined baby's bed. Wasn't this exactly how my life had begun? My first safe place had also been a wicker traveling basket on the other side of the African continent.

Thus began my journey as a mother—fulfilling, exhausting, times of unbelievable joy as well as deep pain. I thought of my own mother who taught me the essentials of childcare.

Because of her example I felt comfortable with my own baby. We named our firstborn Katrine. As I massaged my little daughter's body with olive oil, I thought how Mary must have done the same with baby Jesus.

I was to give birth to four more children. Daniel, David, Stephen, and Ruth soon joined our growing family. They all spent their early years in the child-friendly atmosphere of an African village—where each one was welcomed as a precious gift. Walter's mother came to live with us in 1958 after Walter's father passed away in Leipzig of a sudden heart attack.

When my fifth child, Ruth, was born, the village chief came to congratulate me and said, "You must be the happiest woman in our neighborhood. You have just had a fifth child, and your mother-in-law is living with you." I agreed with him.

From Walter's mother, Mutti, as we called her, I learned the importance of bringing my children to "joy camp." As an experienced and gifted teacher, Mutti often said that children can only thrive in a classroom if it is filled with a joyful atmosphere. I found this to be especially true for my small children in the atmosphere of our home. I wanted above all for my children to feel safe and sheltered. Each one had their favorite toy, pillow, or blanket which gave them a sense of safety and was an extension of mother love for those times when they could not be held. Linus in the comic strip *Peanuts* gave a respectability to the security blanket with which I can identify.

My years of childbearing were among the happiest in my life. Walter was not quite as comfortable in handling our new infant daughter. He feared that he might be too rough or hurt her. As a German he had observed that the care of infants was predominantly the mother's domain, as were kitchen duties and household chores. Yet, he was never one to be trapped into acting a certain way if it didn't make sense. We talked freely and shared openly as we worked at building yet another cross-cultural bridge as parents. How could we mutually support and complement each other in our new roles as mother and father?

Walter had an uncanny sense of seeing the magic in the world of our children. One morning I was upset because he did not respond to Katrine's waking cry while I was busy in the mud-floored kitchen. I walked into the bedroom, curious at what was happening. I hardly believed my eyes. There he sat in front of the bright-eyed child and was writing in our journal! Katrine, who had pulled herself up in her crib, was no longer crying and looked at her father just as intrigued as I did.

"Ingrid dear, listen to what I just wrote," he told me excitedly. "I think this is what our daughter might be wanting to tell us;" and then he read:

In the morning I look like a bride even though I'm still a baby. I pull myself up in my bed and bump into the mosquito net with my little head. It tumbles down over my golden hair like a veil of snow as I wait for the door to open and my Daddy to come in.

"Oh Walter, you see the beauty in the moment, don't you? And sometimes all I see is the necessity." Again I realized how much I loved this man and yet, how different we were.

After five years of working together in Africa, we had our first furlough in the United States. On that journey, while enduring a particularly long plane ride, Walter told me, "The soul is a pedestrian."

"What do you mean, dear?"

"The soul cannot travel by plane," he explained. "It can only go by foot. It will take my soul days to catch up with my body. My body is already in France on its way to America. My soul is still in Africa."

"See, I am sending my angel before you to lead you safely to the land I have prepared for you."
~Exodus 23:20~

This was our promise for the return trip from home leave back to Africa. Daniel was ten months old and Katrine a little over three when we took the Pullman car from Chicago to Washington to New York. Here we boarded the largest and fastest ship of its time, the *SS United States*. In 1957 this was still the cheapest way to get across the Atlantic. Six days later our train for Paris was waiting on the ship's quay in LeHavre. From Paris we took a night train to Karlsruhe in Germany where Walter had just a few days to go over the proofs of our Fulani picture Bible, a project to which we both had devoted much time.

Then back to Paris for our night flight to Africa. We agreed that many protecting angels were necessary when traveling with two small children. Our hands were rarely free to lead little Katrine by the hand, let alone to carry her when she was tired.

A sultry African morning greeted us in Fort Lamy. From there we took yet another plane to Garoua in Cameroun. At that airport our missionary colleague, Ernest Johnson, awaited us with his pick-up truck. Africa had received us again.

We desperately needed to reach the new ferry across the swollen Benoue River before nightfall. Ernest tried to drive as fast as the African road permitted. In vain. A tropical downpour dissolved the road beneath us and turned it into treacherous mud.

We finally arrived at the Benoue crossing at 11 p.m. Too late. The ferrymen did not have to work at night. We flashed our lights across the river and honked our horn, but no signal was returned. Heavy rain kept pounding down. The children were asleep on our laps. We dared not move for fear of waking them.

All of a sudden we heard voices and shouts! The ferry emerged from the darkness. Those faithful people! Despite the rain and the night they had come for us. We crossed the river quickly and without problems. Tchollire was only 25 miles away. Would we reach it tonight?

Our hearts had rejoiced too soon. The back wheels of the pick-up barely missed the hardened tracks of the road and slid into the mud. Ernest tried with all his might to keep the front wheels out. But soon the left front wheel also slipped down into the muck. The truck tilted 45 degrees to the left. We were at a standstill.

The two Africans traveling with us in the back of the truck borrowed our only flashlight and took off to the nearest village. They wouldn't be back in less than four hours. Ernest tried to get some sleep under a tarp in the bed of the pick-up. Because of our precarious angle, Walter and I kept sliding to the left in the truck's cabin and sitting on top of each other. The children had now traveled three nights in a row and were restless. They fell easy prey to mosquitoes.

Finally, at 3 a.m. we heard voices. The faithful ferry operators had come again to help us. Next, we helped unload the entire pick-up. The new day dawned before our wheels were finally on firm ground again. At seven in the morning we drove up to the mission station in Tchollire. What jubilation!

God had sent his angel before us and brought us safely to the land he had prepared for us, just as He had promised at the outset of our trip. We quietly gave Him thanks.

I must admit that it was not always easy to just stay at home and care for the children while Walter led a full and intellectually stimulating life at the college in Libamba. I needed to remind myself of the long-term investment I was making in the children's future. I was a people-maker. This outweighed the importance of any other personal short-term ambitions. Many mothers of young children have found themselves in a similar struggle for balance. It is not a battle that can be won overnight.

Our own children were in pre-school and elementary school when we moved from their birth country in Africa to the hill-country of Upper Austria, which I like to think of as the Ozarks of Europe. Walter wanted his children to have the best continental European education possible. Austria was a wonderful place to raise our three sons and two daughters through their teenage years. In fact, for a few short months we actually had five teenagers.

"Let us educate our children, not so that they will do good—but so that it is impossible for them to do evil."
~George MacDonald~

We dreamed of giving them each a room of their own and their own safe place. Both Walter and I remembered hungering for our own four walls as children. In Austria we certainly could not afford a house large enough to realize this dream. So we asked our dear farming neighbors on the Lichtenberg, the Peternbauerns, to let us build some additional rooms in their granary above their stables. This was where Walter fixed up a study and counseling room for himself and also where the three older children found peace away from the normal commotion of family life.

However, we did insist on sitting down to meals together, and dinners were usually followed by Walter reading out loud from a favorite children's book while I tried to reduce the mending pile by a few items. We both agreed that mealtime conversations were of utmost importance in encouraging the children to express themselves and in getting to know them. It was also a good time for teaching good manners. As one mother said, "Manners are always motivated by thoughtfulness to others, a reminder that we are not the center of the universe." Good manners are caught as well as taught.

We also kept a little *Thank You Box* by the table. Every member of the family could stick little notes of gratitude in it and when the box got too full, Daniel, our oldest son, read the notes out loud while we enjoyed a special dessert. This little box did us good service in tilting the teenager conversation scale away from grumbling towards gratitude.

Individual time with each one of the children also became a priority for me. Whenever possible, I tried to treat each child as an only child. This was not always easy to manage. It was rewarding to carve out an hour alone with each child, whether on a shopping trip or a special walk, at home or away.

Walter was good at having a vision and planning special family times, such as going on camping trips or sharing his love for opera with his children. On a trip through Bavaria, he took eleven-year-old Stephen to see the Opera House in Bayreuth. By chance they were given free tickets to a five-hour dress rehearsal of Wagner's opera *Siegfried*. Although Stephen was not quite able to appreciate Wagner at the time, attending this performance has become one of his most treasured memories of being with his father. Today, opera is Stephen's favorite dramatic art.

Family camping was another story. In some ways it was more strenuous than staying at home, but the rewards were great. As a friend once told me, "The family that camps together, stays together."

On one such memorable venture, we had found a friendly farmer near the Czech border who let us pitch our tents in the middle of his forest. No facilities whatsoever—but "Oh how isolated and romantic and perfect!" Walter exclaimed.

Our oldest was fourteen, and somehow the children managed to pitch their own tent while I struggled to cook our stew on the little camp stove. "Where is the blue water bucket?" I asked. "Children, have you seen the blue water bucket? Wasn't it in the trunk of the car, Walter?"

"I've got it, Ingrid!" he replied, emerging from the little green pup tent that we had rented for Walter and me. "I had to do some emergency construction because we're missing one section of a tent pole."

He proudly opened the tent flap and showed me his makeshift solution to the problem. The existing part of the pole stood upright, precariously balanced on the overturned bucket. By some miracle of physics the tent also stood up-right.

"Daddy, do you think it will stay that way all night?" seven-year-old Stephen weighed in. He was always the most technically minded of our children.

"I guess, we'll have to think of other ways to get our water," was all I had to add.

Night came. I lay down exhausted, barely noticing that our air mattress had already leaked half its air. I was too tired to care after handling the mammoth job of cooking outdoors for my hungry family. Walter leaned over and took my hand, "Isn't this the most wonderful way to bond with our children, Ingrid?"

I wasn't sure it was a good way to bond with my husband, I thought. "Maybe you're right, sweetheart. I just don't feel that wonderful right now," I managed to say. I'd had neither time nor water to wash my face before going to bed. Surely this was no worse than trying to sleep upright in a pick-up truck bogged down on a muddy African road. By the time my thoughts reached Africa, I had fallen fast asleep.

Peels of thunder startled us awake. A gust of wind howled through the treetops. I think our dear little tent decided to capitulate and collapse before the wind even hit it. By then the clouds burst open and rain pelted down on our little wriggling green heap of tarp in the middle of the Austrian woods.

Daniel, our oldest son, was the first to run to our rescue. He and David offered to spend the rest of the night in the car so we could squeeze in with the other children in the second tent. By then everyone involved in the 'rescue-your-parents' mission was thoroughly wet, and Ruthy was awake as well. At three in the morning Stephen began telling us about putting a raw egg on his math teacher's chair who had then promptly sat down on it. Walter and Katrine laughed so loud that Danny and David yelled from the car, "What's so funny?" Stephen repeated his story. More sidesplitting giggles.

Walter was right after all. We were bonding with our children in a wonderful way. Maybe a bit chaotic and unpredictable, but wonderful nonetheless.

As mothers we must give birth to our children many times over in their lifetime. Parenting is never done. There is always one of them who keeps you on your knees. And if it's not your own child, it's a grandchild, a niece or nephew, or a friend's child, as dear to you as your own.

"I have been driven many times to my knees
by the overwhelming conviction
that I had nowhere else to go."
~Abraham Lincoln~

Parents of teenagers can easily identify with Lincoln's words. Adolescence has sometimes been called the "flu of the personality." There were a lot of runny noses, times of fever, and malaise when emotionally our children needed "chicken soup." It helped me to know that this flu time would soon be over and that a magnificent human being was emerging. We tried not to pick on our children constantly but to wrap them in a cocoon of love and acceptance. We practiced much patience too as we watched God at work. The family needed traffic rules. There were consequences when boundaries were not kept. We tried to catch and affirm our young ones when they were doing something right instead of overreacting if they did something wrong.

"Behold, children are an inheritance from the Lord."
~Psalm 127:4~

An inheritance is usually an awesome privilege. God's plan and desire is that our children are precious and should be trained for success. He has called us to prepare them like a skilled craftsman fashions an arrow. God created children to win. He intended them to achieve. Love, not authority, should be the cornerstone of our relationship with our teenagers. Teenagers are children in transition. They are not miniature adults. They need to know that we love and accept them unconditionally.

Walter and I tried to treat our children as persons, not as possessions. We tried not to ridicule or judge them. We tried to respect them and to respect their privacy.

However, as far as guidelines go, it is far easier to write them down now than it was to live up to them back then.

Our children are a tremendous gift, no doubt, but every such gift is also a tremendous responsibility. A friend told me that you are not truly grown up until you have raised at least one child to adulthood. Parenting means more than releasing your child to the world in the morning and expecting him back by nighttime. How easy that would be.

I recall the night before our wedding in Mannheim, Germany when Walter's mother asked to say a word at the rehearsal dinner. "I just want to say," she announced, "that I hereby renounce the first place in the life of my son and give it to Ingrid."

I was quite naive at the time and thought, "Doesn't every mother do that when her son or daughter marries?"

Now it's fifty years later. I have become a mother-in-law five times over. I've experienced the same pain on the wedding day of each of my children—that of knowing I must let them go unconditionally. Just as the umbilical cord must be cut after the birth of a child, if that child is to survive, so I must be willing to cut the cords to my children. Without real leaving there can also be no real homecoming. One doctor put it this way: "Have them! Love them! Let them go!" This leaving, especially of our married children, is an on-going action.

Now I am separated from my adult children and their families, and we can be together only on special occasions. But I have their pictures. In the morning I can pick up a picture, hold that child to my heart, and commit him or her and that day to the Lord before I go about my daily work. The greatest blessing I can give them is to assure them that they are greatly loved.

This chapter is dedicated to our precious children. They are a gift of life to me that keeps on giving. Let me quote from a letter that Walter wrote to Katrine when she was one year old. Father and daughter were separated by continents and Walter was suffering through his first round of life-long leave-takings.

My dear Pimmelpammelchen!

You have crawled through this world for one whole year already. But you do not understand time. And for you every day is as it is: whole, full, free, without constraints tying it to the past, without heavy thoughts that fearfully grope toward the future. You blessed little dot, you don't know time, you don't know length, and you don't know what it means to be bent.

You are so far away. Nations, countries, oceans, continents separate us. But you don't understand space, you blessed little dot, and therefore you don't understand longing and the pain of parting. For you, space is not something that you walk through, but it is something that surrounds you like the love of God. In the middle of that love, all places are equally far away and equally close.

My wish for you is that something of the nature of this first year will always remain with you. Never again will you be so near to eternity, without the limitation of time and place, until the end when everything begins.

Your Father

"It is not only children who feel sheltered in the presence of their mother, but mothers are also sheltered in the presence of their children," Dr. Theo Bovet once comforted me. "It is not parents who make children, but children who make parents."

As I write this life story, I have just held my newborn granddaughter, Kate Marie Trobisch, in my arms. As she looked into my eyes, I saw the wisdom of generations past as well as generations to come. Though she was only a few hours old, I found my heart filling with awe and falling totally in love with her. I thought of Luther's words, "When you see a child, you see Jesus Christ." Jesus told his disciples, "Whoever receives this little one in my name, receives me."

Walter and Ingrid

EIGHT

ON WRITING

"The question is not what you look at but what you see."
~Henry David Thoreau~

Many times as a student and in my various African homes, I had created a special corner for my little typewriter, the Olympia Skywriter. I dreamed of writing the story of my parents and my own childhood one day.

A writer's story begins long before she writes her first word. I remember our modest home at Libamba, in the rain forest in Cameroun. Our Green Prison was completely surrounded by the equatorial virgin forest. Three of our five children were born during our years of living there. My daily routine was centered around their needs and providing a haven of rest for my busy husband.

As soon as feasible, I did set up my little writing corner in our bedroom. I knew that the most I could hope for would be an hour after breakfast when the older children were rested, fed, and content while the baby took her morning nap. Above the desk and the typewriter a narrow bookshelf harbored some of my most treasured books. All my life I have loved to read. Biographies fascinate me in a special way.

At that time I had been reading the so-called missionary classics—biographies of contemporary missionaries and their adventures. During the almost non-existent little breaks in my daily routine I was able to snatch a paragraph here and there. But joy came in the evening after bedtime prayers had been said and the last little squeaky call for water had been answered. I would prop my feet up on the handcarved African stool that remains in our home to this very day.

I noticed that Harper & Row in New York had published these recent missionary biographies. Their address, 49 East 33rd Street, New York 16, was printed inside the cover of each book. Taking all my courage in hand, I wrote to the head of the Religious Department, Mel Arnold. I had learned that one needed to write a letter of query before submitting a manuscript. I also knew that it had to be short. So I wrote a three-paragraph letter to Mr. Arnold telling him that I had a story to tell, what the story was about, and why I thought Harper & Row would be the right publisher.

A month later I received an impressive airmail letter postmarked in New York. I opened it with trembling hands. It was from Mel Arnold and began with the salutation, "Dear Miss Trobisch," That made me laugh since here I was surrounded by five little ones, my baby not even a year old.

"Of course we are interested in your story," Mr. Arnold said. "Please send us an outline of your book and a sample chapter."

I have often met would-be authors who tell me they have a story they would like published and then ask if I could help them. When I say, "May I see what you have written?" the answer is often, "Oh, I haven't written anything yet. It's all in my head."

"Just write it," I tell them.

Now I had to face reality myself and do the same thing myself. I shared the letter excitedly with Walter. He had a busy schedule serving as both the German professor and chaplain at Cameroun Christian College. After reading Mel Arnold's encouraging letter, Walter hugged me and promised to do what he could to help me make my writing project a reality. I could use his office at the back of the college chapel every day from four to six. He would grade his papers at home and at the same time keep an eye on our children. I was thankful for his offer and set to work. After two weeks I had finished the book outline and a sample chapter entitled *The Zamzam* and sent it to New York.

"To write honestly and with all our powers
is the least we can do, and the most."
~Eudora Welty~

More anxious weeks went by as I waited for a reply. Then the letter came. My heart danced as I read Mel Arnold's favorable answer ending with the words, "We are ready to offer you a contract." For almost a decade I had been doing research. I had typed my father's travel journals and letters. I had written to some of the authors I admired, asking for their advice. One of them was Elizabeth Elliot, who had written several missionary classics. In her letter to me dated June 3, 1959, she said:

> *If you decide to write your parent's story, I would advise you to make it as simple as possible. If they have a story to tell, let them tell it— that is, do not try to editorialize. Simplicity is the hardest thing to attain in good writing, but it is worth aiming at.*

Letters went back and forth between New York and Libamba. I asked Mel Arnold how they could offer me a contract when they didn't even know I could write. "We know when we have a good family story," he said, "and we also know how to help you write it. It took us 150 years of publishing history to learn that women read more than men did. That's why we are looking for family stories written by women." He also told me that they only publish one out of 600 unsolicited manuscripts that his publishing house receives annually. He asked how soon I could come to New

York so we could talk face to face... This made me feel apprehensive and honored at the same time.

Our family was due for home leave in a few months. It had been six years since I had seen my family and friends in the United States. Walter suggested I leave Africa a few weeks ahead of him and take our three youngest children with me. We made arrangements for David and Stephen to stay with Mutti, Walter's mother, who was now settled in West Germany.

I arrived in New York in February 1962, with my youngest, Ruth, who was not quite two. A kind friend offered to care for her while I met with Mel Arnold and Edward Sammis who would be my editor for the project. Our two oldest children, Katrine and Daniel, were still in our missionary children's school in Cameroun and would come to Europe with their father at the end of the school year. The plan was that I would finish my book in the States in two weeks and then go back to Germany. Little did I know what lay ahead!

"Every life contains within it a potential for clarification."
~Peter Hoeg~

Filled with joyful anticipation and a sense of incredulity that this was actually happening to me, I walked from my hotel to 49 East 33rd Street in downtown Manhattan. Mel Arnold received me kindly in his office where books covered not only the walls but spilled over on the chairs and floor. He was a tall, imposing Lincolnesque kind of man who focused intently on our conversation and made notes in his little black book. At the end of our visit he handed me a blue legal document—the contract for my book with the working title, *That Thy Way May Be Known*. It was to be an account of how my parents' wedding prayer from Psalm 67 had been dramatically answered.

As I walked back to my hotel room a few blocks away, my heart danced. It was an unbelievable moment, beyond my wildest dreams. I hugged my purse containing the contract. My book was to become a reality, and I had a firm goal. I could only liken it to the certainty I felt when I became engaged and had the letter with Walter's declaration of love in my hands. Such moments stand still in time.

When I first thought of writing the story, it was to be of my father—a biographical account written in the third person. After a few false starts, it became clear that this was the wrong approach. It was stiff and cold. "Try writing it in the first person, as you remember and experienced it," my editor said. I soon found out that he was not nearly as interested in what Father had done on his pioneer journeys, as in what had happened to Mother and us ten children after Father's sudden death in Tanzania during World War II. What I had planned to be the epilogue turned out to be the real story.

I did sign the contract with Harper & Row, promising to have the finished manuscript in their hands by fall, giving me six months instead of two weeks. Walter finished his teaching in Libamba, gathered up Katrine and Daniel from their school in northern Cameroun and David and Stephen from their Grandmother in Germany. He traveled with them to Springfield, Missouri, where I was staying with my mother in our childhood home. Mother helped me with childcare and meal preparation as I struggled through the first chapters of my book.[3]

"If you're trying to write,
you have to let your attention drop.
You can't maintain an interest in anything else."
~Barbara Tuchman~

Editor Sammis had told me to set a pace for myself and write whether I felt like it or not. I found that I could do no more than three typewritten pages daily. He would hold me accountable. Every Saturday I was to send him what I had written and he would evaluate it. Never did this kind, older gentleman, whom I called Uncle Sam, tell me how much work was left to do. Instead he said, "Keep it coming! Keep it coming!" and there would always be a few words of praise.

Friends wrote me wonderfully encouraging letters. Some words by August Herman Francke, one of the fathers of Pietism, truly pushed me on. He said of himself, "I had a joy in fighting, which only increased with difficulties."

I was running an obstacle course of difficulties by trying to balance the roles of wife, mother, and writer. I found myself even fighting with my typewriter. As in childbirth, my clenched fists certainly would not help bring this book to life. Instead I relaxed my breathing and let my hands go limp. I learned to open my hands, ready to receive what God might want to put into them and then transfer it to that empty page in my typewriter—*That Thy Way May Be Known.*

I wrote to Pearl S. Buck whom I admired greatly as an author and who had grown up on the mission field in China. She answered me promptly from her home in Pennsylvania and encouraged me to push on. She was forty when she began writing and produced over sixty books before her death. She was also the first woman to win the Nobel Prize for literature.

In studying her biography *My Several Worlds,* I found out that she didn't enjoy the actual mechanics of writing. She called it "the most tiresome work one can choose." Each day her mind would invent various excuses to prevent her from beginning to write. But she always began "successfully resisting the urge to play the piano, stroll in the sun, work with her flowers, read a book or do any one of a hundred or more things..." She, too, set a pace of three pages a day, and her family knew that even on trips, they could not proceed to their next destination until she had written her quota for the day. She took great pleasure in accomplishment and often said "true joy, real happiness, lies in the completion of a project."

It did take six months before I finished the first draft of my book. I was invited to New York to go through the manuscript with Uncle Sam. It was November 1963. The day Walter and I arrived there was the day President Kennedy was shot. It was difficult to proceed with work as usual, but we tried. For a whole week we sat in Uncle Sam's cozy living room in downtown Manhattan while he, together with his wife, read the manuscript aloud to us, all the while marking it with his red pen. He told us that another of his editing projects was a manuscript by President Kennedy entitled *A Nation of Immigrants*. Kennedy set himself the following guidelines: Every sentence had to either move the story forward or make the reader laugh or cry. If it didn't do one of those three, you cut it out.

Walter and I watched as Uncle Sam did that very thing to my story. Many of my descriptive paragraphs, which I had worked so hard to formulate, he crossed out. "As an author, you must be ready to crucify your darlings," he explained. This was a painful process, but one of the greatest lessons I've learned about writing.

> *"One ought to write only when one leaves a piece of one's flesh in the inkpot each time one dips one's pen."*
> *~Leo Nikolayevich Tolstoy~*

For both of us, this experience of working with Ed Sammis was a valuable apprenticeship. Walter said that he had learned more about effective writing in this week with Uncle Sam than in any university course he had taken.

When we were finished reading my manuscript together, Uncle Sam handed it to me and said, "Now go back home and write it again. You've got the right idea." He also told me that the final choice of a title lies not with the author, but with the publisher. I went back to Springfield and wrote the story a second time. Once more Uncle Sam edited it, and I retyped it. As I think of that painful and slow process forty years ago, I give thanks for God's gift of word-processing for authors today.

The editors were ready to name my book. Instead of the working title taken from Psalm 67, *That Thy Way May Be Known*, a hymn title was chosen, *On Our Way Rejoicing*! Finally my manuscript was ready for Harper's copy editor who checked every historical date and name, asking me questions about anything she felt was unclear. The next step was reading the galley proofs and writing the blurb for the cover: "The trials and triumphs of a close-knit family whose vision led them to the ends of the earth." Several months later I received my first copy of *On Our Way Rejoicing* with its beautiful cover and frontispiece of my birthplace on the slopes of Mt. Kilimanjaro.

What an incredible feeling of accomplishment spread through me as I leafed through the pages! I reread the epilogue, my very own words in print:

> *Writing a book is like climbing a mountain. It can be done only by charting a course, by teamwork, carrying heavy loads, putting one foot in front of the other, heading for the goal.*
>
> *Writing is not only like climbing a mountain—step by step, straight for the goal—but it's also like the birth of a child.*
>
> *There are the months (sometimes years) of carrying the child, still hidden from the world; then the hours of travail. Deep appreciation is here expressed not only to all those on the editorial staff of Harper & Row who watched over this process so carefully, but most of all to the consulting editor, Edward Sammis, the 'Master Obstetrician' without whose help, constant encouragement and professional skill this 'child' would never have come to birth.*

I knew exactly what I needed to do. I sat down at my desk, opened the book and wrote on its first page:

Oct. 1. 1964

Dearest Katrine,

When I was writing one of these chapters, you said to me, "Please, Mommy, will you promise me something? When you are finished with your book, may I have the very first copy?"

I promised you then that I would, because it was of you, your brothers and sister, and cousins that I was thinking as I wrote down this story.

So here it is, just for you, my oldest daughter and the answer of many prayers, the very first copy!

With love,

Your mother

That was the beginning of our writing ministry, with its ever-widening circles. Next came Walter's book, *I Loved a Girl*, a private correspondence between him and one of his African students with its frank questions about the difference between lust and love. It was soon translated into more than fifty languages and published throughout the world. Walter said, "First I wrote the book and then the book wrote my life."

We received an avalanche of letters from readers—especially from African countries. As we conscientiously answered these letters, new books were born. Walter wrote *I Married You*, and I wrote *The Joy of Being a Woman*. These books in turn became the foundation for our teaching and retreat ministry which we called Family Life Mission or FLM.

We were invited to hold Family Life Seminars throughout the world. In September 1979 we returned to our home on the Lichtenberg in Austria from a three-month teaching trip around the world. We were weary but filled with joy as we saw the rich fruits from our ministry. Our children were taking their first steps into adulthood. As a couple we looked forward to the next stage of our life together—that of the empty nest.

Our books, by then more than a dozen, were rapidly being published in the major languages of the world. My German editor, Elisabeth Wetter, when asked in an interview what is necessary today to be a good author, answered:

"A good author must be able to put into words what she thinks, so that it will be understood. She must stay aware of what is happening today as well as see through what is happening. She should have a message that makes sense to her readers and that they are ready to accept."

Our books were meeting these criteria if the echoes we received from our readers were a good gauge. Willa Cather, Pulitzer-Prize winning author, says there are only five stories to tell: birth, decision-making, love, suffering, and death—just as birds have only five distinctive notes in their songs.

We had written about the first three. Then, with Walter's sudden death in 1979, our world together came to an end. Now it was my turn to write about suffering and death.

It took five years before I was able to share my experiences of learning to walk alone after Walter's death and another five before I could write my message, especially for women, on how to live confidently in a world full of stress and put-downs.

An important secret of that confidence is having a place of one's own. And so I told my own story of Haus Geborgenheit, the *House of Steadfast Shelter*. The book was entitled *Keeper of the Springs*, with the subtitle *Making Home the Place for Which You are Longing*.

I have found, as did Anne Lindbergh, that the key to effective writing is a moment of insight, like seeing a distant landscape. And yet every time I sit down at my desk, I struggle to find the right words. I look around for the wisdom of others who could do it so much better than me. Reading about their insights gives much more pleasure than formulating my own.

Sometimes in my frustration, all I want to do is to hit the computer's DELETE key. (The old Olympia Skywriter has long been relegated to a corner in the attic.) Interruptions breed more interruptions while I desperately try to concentrate. However, the power of my own wishful thinking does not produce one real word on the blank screen in front of me. When interrupted by a phone call, my mind makes wonderful excuses for not going back to the writing project at hand. Then suddenly, amidst all this formidable confusion, I hear the still, small voice of my Gentle Shepherd saying, "Just tell your story, Ingrid, and leave the rest to me."

It has been especially difficult for me to write my own story. Even the reasons for that difficulty are hard for me to put into words. Perhaps I have lived the equivalent of three lives when it comes to volume of experience and travel. Or maybe looking on as an objective observer is foreign to me when it comes to putting my own life into words. I would much rather live life than write about it.

"It is hard to write about the life one is actually living."
~Robert Finch~

My editor gives me the following advice: "Don't ask your reader, 'Who am I?' but tell him who you are. Write down your own experiences because every experience is like a seed or kernel from which energy radiates in various directions. Let the story speak for itself. No philosophizing or preaching or lecturing. You don't have to tell your reader what to think. Nor does the reader like being told what to think."

Lew Smedes, author and friend, wrote to me:

"Writing your autobiography, are you? A splendid project, not only because your life has been a fascinating adventure, but because your memory of it and your examination of it ('the unexamined life is not worth living'—though surely worth having been lived) will help all to

*be the more thankful for you and help the favored among us to add
thanks for your friendship to us. Bless you in the project on the revis-
iting of yourself.*

*Have you considered letting someone write your biography instead?
Though I trust your wisdom, insight, and candor, I fear your modesty
will shadow your achievements. But you must do it—above all
this—your chosen way."*

When a dear friend read these words recently, he said,
"Amen! Lew Smedes is right about the danger of your modesty shadowing your achievements. Ingrid, I love you for your
humility, but I also long to encourage and help you realize
your achievements." What a mighty cheering section I have!

It is significant that there are the events that I remember
amidst all the others I can't bear to remember. However, in
the end, I write in order to see and feel more clearly, in order
to hold onto past events that are dear to me. Recently my siblings shared what they remembered of the day we heard the
news of my father's death. Each one of us had completely
different memories of the same event. No wonder I am be-
fuddled when trying to come up with a clear line of thought
for an event that happened so long ago and yet affected us so
deeply and in such diverse ways.

*"I must write it all out, at any cost.
Writing is thinking. It is more than living,
For it is being conscious of living."
~Anne Morrow Lindbergh~*

Life is messy. Therefore an honest autobiography will have to
be messy. The author cannot afford to paint his or her life
picture in clearly defined shades of black and white. Mud will
have to be part of the color scheme. It takes courage to be
truthful. Life is a mystery to be lived, not a problem to be

solved. "Be open to surprises," one editor told me. "Don't applaud yourself, but don't minimize yourself either."

Another thing I have learned is that our battles speak louder than our victories. One of my greatest struggles as a busy wife, mother, and speaker has been to find my *quiet center* and write from that. The problem is not only to find the room of one's own and the time to use that room, but it is even more "how to still the soul in the midst of its activities," as Anne Lindbergh said.

To write well one must relax and get rid of the mental clutter. Soul and spirit must be together. I have to write this story first of all for myself—to make sense out of my life, and second to pass on a legacy. Something in me has to die, so that something else can live. Life is an ongoing voyage of self-discovery—coming into possession of new land.

I just watched a documentary on the life of Eleanor Roosevelt. At the end, the narrator stated that Eleanor's life had been one of constant discovery, but the greatest discovery she had made was the discovery of herself. I want to personally articulate what I learn on my voyage of self-discovery, for that brings much happiness. However, my greatest happiness will always be "to know Him and enjoy Him forever."

Journaling and letter writing are my favorite forms of writing.

Journaling is not simply keeping a diary and listing all of my activities. Rather it is a personal record of how what has happened has affected me.

My desk drawers are filled with journals. These journals have become a way of "tying my fragmented life together," as my daughter Katrine would say. They provide "a shelter for my hopes, dreams, faith, and for the love with which I live my life."

Katrine, whose husband is a U.S. diplomat, has enjoyed teaching spiritual journaling classes throughout the world. She has greatly encouraged me in my journaling adventures and in helping me choose themes for each new journal. This is how she explains journaling to her students:

It is a human need to somehow keep a record of our lives. The more fragmented the life, the deeper the need. A journal is a book about our daily journey. It will never be completed. It will never be perfect. If you start your book with this in mind, you are already on the right path. Have courage to write about the little steps even when they seem incoherent and haphazard. The rest will fall into place.

I also spend hours each week writing letters. Personal correspondence was an essential part of Walter's ministry. His first book, *I Loved a Girl,* is an exchange of personal letters which has spoken to hearts all over the world. Katrine writes in our book, *Keeper Of The Springs:*

There are many kinds of letters, including the obligatory and those you can't wait to sit down and write. In letters you explore the landscape of your soul and reveal it to a friend... Even the envelope is lovingly addressed by hand, the stamp carefully chosen and placed. It's easy to sift these letters from the daily avalanche of mail and patiently wait for the first uninterrupted moment to open such a treasure. Reading it is like opening a window with a striking view. What a luxury to think a thought to the end with pen and paper!

Even now I find it hard work to write. I have that same sensation which John Steinbeck called "a miserable sick feeling of inadequacy" when it's time to write. But then when the words are on paper, I am fulfilled and at peace.

Ingrid and Katrine at Walter's funeral

NINE

GRIEF

Grief is the price you pay for loving.

The day is October 13, 1979. Walter opens the drapes in the bedroom of our little home on the Lichtenberg in the foothills of the Austrian Alps. Radiant morning sunshine pours in. A few late roses bob their heads in the breeze right outside our window. The mountain air is crisp and cool. Each time it refreshes me anew after our years of living in the tropics.

"I'll be right back with the tea tray," Walter tells me as I luxuriously turn over and stretch in our own bed. We had just arrived home after a three-month missionary trip that had taken us around the world. It was Saturday and three of our children, Daniel and his fiancée Betty, Stephen, and Ruth would be home for the weekend. Ruth, our youngest, had just had her eighteenth birthday, and today we would celebrate it as a family. I had wrapped her little birthday gifts yesterday evening as Walter read a chapter to me from John White's book, *Parent in Pain*. Walter told me how thankful he was for each child and that today he wanted to write each one of them a letter.

Now he entered our bedroom carrying the tea tray with the little white china teapot, two cups, and a piece of whole wheat toast which he had cut in two pieces and spread with red currant jam. He had already showered and shaved and was wearing his maroon dressing gown given to him by the father of one of his African students in Cameroun many years ago. He put the tray down on my bedside table and said matter-of-factly, "Ingrid, my body is trying to tell me something, but I don't understand it."

He took his place in the bed beside me, propped up by pillows as I poured his cup of tea. We were going to read the Watchword for the day from the Moravian Daily Texts. I heard him gasp for breath and managed to take his teacup before it spilled. I called his name and tried mouth-to-mouth resuscitation. No response. I hurried to the phone and called our village doctor who arrived within minutes.

"It's too late," Dr. Greil told me. "The walls of his heart have broken."

My world reeled to a stop at that moment.

I called out to our Austrian neighbors, Matthias and Ernie, whose farmhouse was only 50 yards away. They embraced me silently and said they would call the village pastor and our children, Daniel and Ruth, in Salzburg. Somehow I managed to call Stephen in Vienna, David in Heidelberg, and Katrine in Richmond, Virginia. And then I was alone with him. Time stood still as I knelt at his side and prayed. I saw a change come over his face. It was a look of transfigured peace, almost as if he were smiling secretly. Heaven was very near in our little bedroom that October morning. "A sudden death is a kiss of God," St. Augustine once said.

I was numb with shock. I knew the pain would come later, so now I had to be strong and make the right decisions. Matthias and Karl, another of our farmer neighbors, helped me dress Walter while his body was still warm. I chose his best white shirt that I had just washed the day before. "Put it in my small black suitcase," he had said. "Then it's ready for my next journey." We chose his silver tie—the one he always wore for weddings and special celebrations—and his favorite dark suit.

Our Austrian pastor arrived. He prayed at Walter's bed-side, together with all the neighbors from the four families on the Lichtenberg who had come to grieve with me. Then Matthias said he would go to the little town of St. Georgen, notify the funeral director and pick out a simple pine coffin.

I picked up the little booklet of Moravian Daily Texts that still lay on Walter's bedside table. Now I read the text we were preparing to read together as he took his last breath.

Steadfast love and faithfulness will meet;
Righteousness and peace will kiss each other.
Psalm 85:10

Rejoice in your hope, be patient in tribulation, be constant in prayer.
Romans 12:2

I couldn't grasp either one of them at the moment. I remembered that two days earlier, during our quiet time together, we had read the words, "I will turn your mourning into joy" (Jeremiah 31:13), and the answering verse in the New Testament, "Blessed are those who mourn, for they shall be comforted" (Matthew 5:4).

How much of Walter's life had been spent in journeying—and yet he was at home in his own bed when he died. One of his friends, a vineyard keeper in Germany wrote to me on his card of condolence, "Walter was a laborer in God's vineyard. He died in the middle of the grape harvest."

I sat alone in my grief. I had no sense of time. Then I heard a car pull up in our gravel driveway and the next moment quick steps in the hallway. It was our third son, Stephen, who was a freshman at the University of Vienna. His roommate had driven Stephen's old car at breakneck speed the 200 miles from Vienna. They were the first ones to arrive. Stephen and I embraced in silence, and then he went into our room to weep over his father.

Before long Daniel arrived with our youngest daughter Ruth, whose eighteenth birthday we had planned to celebrate that day. I gave her the card that her father had written to her about coming of age.

My dear Ruth,

The Watchwords for your birthday on September 12th are not relaxing ones—to put you at ease. 'Who can stand the day of His coming?' (Malachi 3:2) and 'God will not show mercy when He judges the man who has not been merciful' (James 2:13). In German 'Barmherzigkeit' (mercy) means to 'carry with your heart.' This is quite a life program for your coming of age. I do not know what your future will look like. The secret of a fulfilled life, however, is to let yourself be carried by the heart of God. Only from there can you gain strength to carry others with your heart.

I went for a walk with Stephen and Ruth after I gave them a cup of tea from the little teapot that their father had placed at my bedside. We walked down the rutted mountain road that Walter and I had walked together the day before. I put my arms around them as we sat on our favorite bench, and I told them all I could remember of my last hours with their father.

"In the midst of life we are in death."
~The Book of Common Prayer~

David and his fiancée Vera arrived from Heidelberg in the late afternoon. We gathered at Walter's bedside. Daniel read the prayer of committal in our Lutheran hymnal, and we sang together in German *Jesus, Still Lead On*. We closed with our family prayer from Psalm 67:1-2, "May God be merciful to us and bless us! May his face shine on us, that his way may be known upon the earth and his salvation among all nations."

Then they came and took his body away—the last farewell from the home he loved so dearly. It was his final journey on this earth.

Five days later Walter was buried beside his mother in the little Alpine cemetery, surrounding the church in Attersee where he had often preached during our fifteen years in Austria. The service was a celebration of his life. Inscribed on the family tombstone were the words, "When morning came, Jesus stood at the shore" (John 21:4).

Two weeks later—All Saints Day—our congregation gathered in the beautiful Austrian churchyard and sang a hymn to honor our departed ones. With tears streaming down my cheeks, I stood at Walter's flower-covered grave. I can still smell the fragrance of that moment. My neighbor Matthias stood beside me. I felt Walter's presence between us, his arms around our shoulders. It was as if he told us that he was not in the grave, and we should not be sad. His journey on earth was ended, but he now had a better home.

I knew then that I had not lost Walter—he was safe at home. But I had lost myself. My long pilgrimage as a widow had just begun.

The letters kept pouring in from all around the globe. This man, who had such a hard time shedding tears himself, was now being wept for by so many who had loved him. Katrine and her three-month-old daughter Virginia came to be with me the first weeks after Walter's death. When she arrived after her long voyage across the Atlantic, Katrine gently placed her baby on Walter's empty pillow. "Look, mother, here is new life!"

I appreciated Katrine's help with the piles of mail. She composed a family letter in response to the many deeply felt expressions of condolence.

My heart was not yet ready to grasp all the words of comfort and sympathy. I just hung on to the refrain of a song by the St. Louis Jesuits:

Be not afraid!
I go before you always.
Come, follow me,
And I will give you rest.

I could take the "next indicated step" as my brother Carl had advised me. Mourning, according to Glen Davidson, is a process that takes you on the journey from where you were before loss to where you will be as you struggle to adapt to change in your life. I learned that there are physical rules that will help us in this process:

A balanced diet which includes fresh fruit and vegetables.
Enough liquid—wonderful cups of herbal tea helped me.
Enough rest.
Exercise each day.
A circle of friends who surround you with caring, nurturing love.

At Christmas all the children came home, and we celebrated the wedding of Betty and Daniel in the village church. The sounds of mourning were turned to songs of joy at this happy event. Yet, I still had the feeling that our family boat had capsized. The captain was gone, and we, the family members, were bobbing around in the water. We each had our life jackets on and could reach out to each other—but we were all headed in different directions. Beyond immediate survival I had no goal.

I was blessed to have strong role models as I entered this difficult and challenging time. Both my grandmother and mother had to raise large families after the too-early deaths of their husbands. I was now a single mother of two teenagers and three children in their early twenties. This gave me a strong sense of purpose, and I identified with Bettina von Arnim, a German mother whose husband, a nobleman, had died in a Russian prison camp. Left alone to raise her six children, Bettina von Arnim had written:

Do not be sorry for me, dear brothers.
I am his wife and have carried his children under my heart.
Much treasure is in these children.
A while yet I shall remain with them,
And this test shall again wed me to him.

Three months after Walter's death, I went to the United States for his memorial service at Augustana Lutheran Church in Minneapolis. As I flew over the clouds between New York and Minneapolis in late January 1980, I watched the glory of the setting sun. It took a long time for the sun to go down because I was flying with the sun. After the sun disappeared, there still was a long stream of golden light. I read a note from a missionary in Indonesia written to me after Walter's sudden death:

Walter's ministry in Indonesia was like the last burst of sunlight—a last fulfillment of his calling. Two thousand Christians from the 800 islands of Indonesia had come together for a week to hear his message on love and marriage. This is the essence of what he said:

The existence of love means working on love. Deep marital love has to be filled with divine love. If you are no longer close to God, you cannot be close to each other. A pastor, who is so busy that he has no time for his wife, sins.

The physical aspects of marriage are just as holy as the legal and personal aspects. Man began with a body in the biblical story of creation and will end with a new body according to the last chapter in the Bible.

There is a sex wave sweeping around the world, much like the tidal wave caused by a volcanic eruption on the ocean floor which just hit one of your islands. The reason for this sex wave is because we Christians do not dare to speak or preach about sex. "One flesh" means not only the physical union, but also it means sharing our thinking and feelings, plans, joys and worries.

This means we have to talk to each other. Talking also means listening. There is only one door through which the feeling of love can enter a woman's heart and that is through her ear. We men especially have to learn to express our love in words. Ephesians 5:21 begins with the mutual submission to Christ. We cannot submit if we do not accept and value ourselves. The husband is only the head of the wife in the same measure that he is her servant, as Christ demonstrated in John 13.

Walter's last sentence before this great audience reflected something of his commission for life: "The testimony of the Christian family is the most effective landing place for the gospel." This is what he tirelessly proclaimed.

As I continued my flight, I thought of the 27 years I had been privileged to walk by his side. I remember the day I had walked down a lonely road in Poli in northern Cameroun when God had made it clear to me beyond a doubt that Walter was to be my husband. And then, two years later, we had been married.

It had not been an easy life. There had been much brokenness and suffering. There were many unfulfilled desires. There were the times when I thought I couldn't keep up with his quick strides—just as I had tried to run as a child to keep up with my father. I was often out of breath and ready to give up—like the evening before our last missionary journey around the world. More than anything else, I had wanted to throw my suitcase out the window and stay at home and rest.

Now, as I sat in the plane watching the golden sky become gray and muted, I saw the first evening star shining brightly above the clouds. I had a letter in my hands from the Secretary of the Indonesian Church. He began with the words from Daniel 12:3, "Those who have taught many people to do what is right will shine like the stars forever."

Was Walter such a star? The thought deeply comforted my broken heart. At Walter's funeral in Austria, one of the leaders of the German Church had said the same thing—that his writing and teachings shone like a star in the moral darkness of present-day Europe.

It is not up to us to judge the effectiveness of our ministry. I can only say, as Walter's wife and companion of 27 years, that he practiced what he preached. Like Martin Luther, it was unthinkable for him not to have a spiritual counselor to whom he himself could go when his heart was burdened with some disobedience. Like Bonhoeffer, he did not believe in cheap grace. He believed it cost more to confess one's sins to God in front of a brother, who could then pronounce the absolution, than to deal with them alone.

Walter had done this himself as a student of theology in his seventh semester at Heidelberg University. After examining his heart in the light of the Ten Commandments, Walter confessed his sins to a brother in Christ. This man pronounced God's Word of forgiveness to Walter who returned to his room with a joyful heart. There Walter found a young man asking for the same spiritual help.

This experience of forgiveness and absolution became the key to his ministry wherever he was. He often said about his book, *I Loved a Girl*, that the secret of its wide appeal was the passage where he invited Francois to repair his telephone wire with God.

For him the secret of a happy marriage had much to do with a healthy self-love and feeling of self-worth on the part of each partner. He loved to point out Ephesians 5:25 and 28, "Husbands, love your wives as Christ loved the church and gave himself for it... He who loves his wife loves himself." Only respect for oneself can bring about respect for one's partner.

During our last journey overseas Walter and I visited the home of a well-known Christian couple. The wife was very active in the pro-life movement, and her husband was a university professor. Both worked hard—for themselves and for their five children—yet there was something missing. When we were alone, Walter said to me, "She doesn't love herself, does she?"

This healthy self-acceptance—being able to laugh at one's own mistakes—was a part of Walter's being. He worked hard, and yet, he was very creative in his enjoyment of life. "If you can't do anything good for yourself, how can you do it for others?" was one of his last written messages to me that I found again after his death.

Winston Churchill writes in a wonderful little book entitled *Painting as a Pastime*, that human beings are divided into two classes: first, those for whom work is work; and second, those for whom work and hobby are one. For them work becomes joy. Most people are in the first category, but as Churchill writes, "Fortune's favored children belong to the second class. Their life is a natural harmony. For them the working hours are never long enough. Each day is a holiday…" When I shared this thought with Walter, he said, "Then I'm one of the fortunate second category. For me, my work is my hobby and my hobby is my work."

Very often in our ministry together, people told us, "What you have to say is not so extraordinary or revolutionary—but the fact that you say it together as a couple impresses us."

I recall the last time we gave a lecture together. We spoke to several hundred students at the large university auditorium in Port Moresby, New Guinea. Walter shared with them how, four years earlier after we had conducted several marriage seminars for others, it became clear to us that we needed help in our own marriage. We registered for a Marriage Encounter weekend in Minneapolis in 1975. In the course of 48 hours, we did more sharing of our deep feelings than we had done for years. The first question given us to write down in our dialogue notebooks was, "Why did you come?" Walter's answer, "In order to learn new things to help other couples." My answer, "In order to learn how we can work on our own marriage."

When I thought of this, I had to smile through my tears. There were many times when I could echo what Winnie Mandela said in an interview about her marriage with Nelson Mandela, "I felt like the most unmarried married woman." This happened especially when Walter was absorbed in a new manuscript. I would call him to lunch. He came and absent-mindedly ate what I had prepared, mentally still preoccupied with his writing. Suddenly, at the end of the meal, he would become aware of where he was and ask, "Have we already eaten?"

And yet I remembered how Walter was always ready to listen to me, no matter how many times he had heard my grievances. He assured me, "I can do nothing without you, Ingrid. You are in every page I write—in every message I prepare."

When I asked a successful African pastor why so many people came to him for help, his answer was, "I just listen to a man, and he's half healed." Walter certainly understood that secret. Being able to listen to men and women alike was indeed one of his gifts.

Whenever possible, we listened together to God's Word and His voice.

"Four ears can hear better than two," Walter said. He cared what I thought and felt, and had deep respect for the gift of a woman's intuition and her feeling for what was right. He made great sacrifices so that I could receive the same training as he did. One summer vacation he took our three older children on a prolonged camping trip so that I could take a concentrated course in marriage counseling in California.

He knew it was harder to do this work together than if he went on a teaching trip alone. Rarely did we set out on such a trip together without experiencing some kind of crisis, either physical or spiritual. Our spiritual mentor told us, "This is a sign that what you are doing is real."

One thing we have observed is that husbands and wives have different rhythms of waking and sleeping. One is a lark, ready to get going early—sometimes even before daybreak. The other is an owl who has a hard time recognizing the end of the day. In our marriage Walter was the lark and I was the owl. It was his joy, after rising early and writing at his desk for a couple of hours, to prepare a tea tray and bring it to our bedroom so that we could begin the day together.

Often, when the door opened and he brought the tray to me, I could picture Jesus as he stood on the shore waiting for the return of his disciples. "When morning came, Jesus stood at the shore" (John 21:4). What was Christ doing for his tired, discouraged friends? He was making breakfast. So Walter did on the last morning of his life—it was his last gesture of love—to hand me the tray he had prepared, lie down himself, and take his last breath. That is why I chose this verse for his tombstone.

My plane was soon to land. Who would be there to meet me? I felt a ball of pain. I remembered the last time I had traveled across continents by myself to Port Moresby in Papua, New Guinea. Walter was waiting with open arms to greet me. He had lovingly prepared every detail for my arrival. Never again would that happen. I thought of what Henri Nouwen had said in *The Wounded Healer*, "No man can stay alive when nobody is waiting for him. Everyone who returns from a long and difficult trip is looking for someone waiting for him at the station or the airport."

Like Nouwen I had viewed the world through the eyes of the one to whom I could tell my story. Now the ever-present dialogue with Walter had come to an end. I would be in a society that is more inclined to help you hide your pain than to grow through it. I thought of the study published in the Minneapolis Tribune after the Vietnam War, asking people how long it is normal to mourn the death of a loved one. The overwhelming majority thought that individuals should be done with mourning between forty-eight hours and two weeks after a death!

I thought of how the disciples of Jesus kept themselves isolated from people for forty days after His ascension, trying to comprehend what had happened. The long period of mourning was necessary before they were able to receive the Spirit. Only after letting their deep pain hurt were they able to receive the great consolation their Lord had promised them. Only after they stopped clinging to their Lord, could his Spirit fill their hearts.

The more I let the *deep pain hurt*, the more I realized that something new was about to be born.

Twenty years later, I sit and write this in my little cabin by the forest in the Ozark Mountains. I start a fire in the fireplace and watch a dry log burn. There is a scar where a branch has been cut off. The flames pour through it. That's like the scar in my life, I contemplate. When Walter left so quickly so many years ago, it was like an amputation. The bleeding has stopped, the wound has healed, and I have learned to walk again, albeit with a limp. "In love's battles, only the wounded can serve," Thornton Wilder has said. Is that why the flame pours out so brightly where the branch has been severed?

Haus Geborgenheit, Springfield, Missouri

TEN

COMING HOME

"To have roots in one's own place
is to be the more able to enter into real communion
with all the other places in the world."
~Paul Tournier~

In the second summer after Walter's death I flew from Salzburg to Springfield to visit my 82-year-old mother. Together we walked down the road to see our long-time neighbors, the Crightons, in their old stone farmhouse. Mrs. Crighton had been my beautiful grade school teacher who at that time so obligingly kissed one of her young pupils "when he sure did need a kiss." Now she was well over seventy.

"We will need to sell this wonderful old house," she told us. "My husband cannot climb the steps anymore." Her next question caught me by complete surprise, "Ingrid, wouldn't you consider buying it?"

At first the idea hit me as preposterous. "Flo, I really can't think of moving. I am a widow and need to help my college-age children finish their education. Austria is their home. I also feel closer to Walter there."

My mother stood by in her thoughtful way. She never spoke more than she had to. She was just there and must have witnessed my first flickering of doubt. Had I answered too hastily? The house was built in 1919, one of its kind. Together we three women walked through each room of the house. Flo had taken care to retain the home's original simplicity and solidness. The furnishings reflected an air of the French provincial style and were accented by floral wallpapers and blue wool carpeting. The worn antique sofa in the formal upstairs living room seemed to call out a personal welcome to me, "Come, sit down and rest, Ingrid. It's all right." I was overwhelmed by the impact the house had on me. "Come on, Mother, let's go home," I said. The house was beginning to talk to me, and I was not ready to listen.

Before I returned to Austria, I phoned Mrs. Crighton, "Flo, I will pray and consider the possibility of buying your home. There is nothing I can promise, but I will let you know one way or the other."

By letter, I shared the thought with my family. John, my older brother, wrote: "What fond memories I have of the old Crighton home! May those sturdy stone walls now house a home which will be a blessing and a beacon of faith to coming generations." And from my other siblings and friends I heard similar strong words of encouragement.

Back in Austria, I spent much time with my children who still lived there. They were by now each striking out in their own life's direction. My youngest daughter, Ruth, had just begun her medical training at the University of Vienna. The thought of leaving her was painful in itself. The thought of pulling up my Austrian roots was almost more than I could bear.

Ruth reassured me and said, "It's the right way. Leave the old burdens behind and enjoy the new beginning. I'm sure many women will envy your decision to establish a new *place* at this time. I am proud of my mother, her example, and her obedience."

Katrine was not quite so encouraging. Because of her frequent moves as a diplomat's wife, she felt I was leaving the only consistent home she knew. My three sons agreed they wanted me to do what I thought best.

One morning in July 1981, I awoke to yet another beautiful sunrise over the Alpine peaks surrounding the Lichtenberg. The fog had receded from the valleys, so I could clearly see Lake Attersee, the beautiful Austrian lake on whose shores Walter lay buried. For the first time I was filled with a quiet, inner assurance that my heavenly Father was leading me back home to Springfield, Missouri, where I had been a child myself. I also knew that He would show me the next steps.

Where would the money come from? Slowly the way became clear. Two German Christian businessmen offered me interest-free loans to make the down payment. I sensed that my time in Europe was coming to an end. Something exciting and new was happening. But first I had to go through a birth process. Like a seed placed in the earth, I had to struggle and gather all my energy to burst through the soil.

In the years since Walter's death, I had often sighed over the cumbersome European bureaucracy. The German authorities even questioned Walter's original certificate of death issued in Austria. It had to be re-issued in Germany. Every interaction required an official and notarized piece of paper. Even putting up his gravestone was an ordeal in fighting the battle of petty regulations. Did everything have to be so complicated? I often had the feeling of being forced inside a too-tight box with the lid closed down on me—the way a baby must feel before the hour of birth.

"With knowledge we begin the journey.
Only by love do we reach the end."
~Katrine Stewart~

My thoughts swam in wild currents with few resting places. As long as Walter was at my side, I had felt at home wherever we lived. But now on this spectacular morning, after more than three decades of voluntary *exile*, the assurance came that I was free to leave and go back to my roots.

I reread some old letters that Walter wrote as a young man, trying to explain his call to Africa to our mission board. He said that he heard his first call when he was thirteen years old while listening to the St. Matthew's Passion by Bach. Since Walter's death, music had comforted my open wound of grief more than anything else. I learned to stop the bleeding points as I listened again to the simple song of the St. Louis Jesuits:

> *Be not afraid!*
> *I go before you always.*
> *Come follow me,*
> *And I will give you rest.*

They too seemed to beckon me across the ocean. After all, St. Louis itself was the *Gateway to the West*, the first crossing of the mighty Mississippi, the place of new life for the pioneers and of freedom from tyranny. Perhaps I would find a new freedom too.

> *"Holiness is wholeness."*
> *~Anonymous~*

No. Life did not have to be complicated. "Life is light above the clouds," I wrote in my journal as my plane headed westward.

> *I'm on my way home. I think of Homer's Odyssey. 'As the men came home from Troy, all the lamps were lit.' As I journey home after being in Africa and Europe for 33 years I feel those lighted lamps within. I have to leave four of my children and Walter's grave behind. All I am taking with me are the candlesticks that have symbolized our home, a few vases and pictures, the quilt my grandmother made for me, my journals and special books."*

An unusual fatigue took hold of me right there in my cramped seat on the airplane. I let go of all I was leaving behind. It was no longer my concern. My children were old enough to manage on their own and look after our home on the mountain. They were even old enough to let me go. Now I had to let myself go. I cannot recall the last time I slept so deeply on a plane.

In one of his wonderful novels, George MacDonald writes:

> *In some families the games of the children mainly consist in the construction of dwellings of this kind or that—castle or ship or cave or wood-fort or nest in a treetop—according to the material attainable. It is an outcome of the aboriginal necessity for shelter, this instinct of burrowing. Northern children cherish in their imaginations the sense of protection more than others do. This is partly owing to the severity of their climate, the snow and wind, the rain and sleet, the hail and darkness they encounter.*

I knew that I was looking for this shelter. In one of my suitcases was a carved wooden plaque, the precious handmade gift of a friend. Haus der Geborgenheit it read. *The House of Steadfast Shelter.* It was to be the name of my new home.

But I knew I was looking for something else too. My oldest son, Daniel, a life-long student of father-daughter relationships, said to me as I was leaving our little home in the Alps, "Mother, don't go back to your childhood home, expecting to find your father."

I pondered his words and thought of the book *A Late Friendship* that Walter and I had read aloud together. The book was a collection of letters between the theologian Karl Barth and the German playwright Carl Zuckmayer. In the concluding chapter, Zuckmayer pays tribute to his friend who died shortly before his 82nd birthday, "… I myself had found once again what all of us most need if we are to know ourselves: a father figure."

Yes, my father had left us 40 years ago. He would not come back to me. Nor would Walter. I had to learn to con-

tinue on my journey alone. For the first time in my life I also
had the assurance I could do it.

My plane landed in Washington D.C. where my oldest daughter met me. Her husband, David Stewart, had been appointed
to the U.S. Foreign Service. They now had three young children and would soon be leaving for their first assignment in
Bucharest, Romania. It seemed like our lives were criss-
crossing above the Atlantic. David and Katrine sold me their
old car for $750, a dark green 1971 Chrysler Newport they
affectionately called Nelly. The car's trunk and back seat were
large enough to contain all my suitcases and airfreight, that
part of my old home which was to belong to my new home.

"Mother, you can do it!" were Katrine's last words before
I embarked on my three-day trip.

I was terrified at the prospect of turning onto the George
Washington Parkway and then taking the Beltway out of our
daunting capital. All I had known for many years were dirt
roads in Africa, winding Austrian mountain roads, and the
Autobahn. This was entirely different. I knew that courage
consists not in the absence of fear, but in taking action despite fear. I also knew that friends and family were praying
for me that morning, but I had to take the first step.

I had to turn the ignition key, step on the gas, and steer.

When I crossed the Maryland State line and read *Drive
Gently*, I knew I had passed my first major test. Navigating the
roads of our Capital's metropolis is not something for the
faint-hearted. I drew a deep breath and relaxed. From now
on, highway signs leading west were all I needed to follow.

Rich noonday sun clearly defined every bit of the highway
in front of me. Almost like in a dream, I found myself driving
through mountainous and green West Virginia. Could this be
real? Nelly kept her enormous hood pointed straight towards
the West.

I was driving home. The home of my childhood. The
place where my mother now lived after her years in Bolivia.
The place where my sister Eunice and her family had settled

down after years of missionary service in Pakistan. The place where I had been a little girl before my father died.

Yet I was on another journey this spring morning in late April 1982. This one was different from the others up till now. Usually I had needed to brace myself for all the new that awaited me at journey's end. This time I was going back to what was old and familiar. Absentmindedly I turned on the car radio. For a moment the announcer's fluent American English puzzled me. After so many years of hearing and speaking German, I had come to think that all radios spoke German. How wonderful to understand every single word without straining!

As I crossed the border into Kentucky, I felt the box, into which my soul had been pressed, spring open. An exhilarating sense of freedom took hold of me.

I was on my way home, back to my roots.

It took three days to reach the Ozarks.

Instead of growing more and more tired, my senses seemed to wake up as I neared my home state. On the evening of the third day, about one hour outside of Springfield, I called my mother. I sensed the relief in her voice when she heard where I was. She had been very concerned about my driving alone from the East Coast. After all the years away from her, it felt strange and wonderful to me that she should be so concerned.

I turned off the interstate, drove down Springfield's Battlefield Road, and then turned onto Blackman Road. As I steered Nelly up the tree-lined driveway of the homestead, I remembered my jubilant departure down that very driveway as a thirteen-year-old. Father was then taking me to live with my beloved Grandmother. Both were no longer with me, yet they seemed to be cheering me on. I saw a figure walking toward me with open arms. My mother did not run, for that was not like her, but her strides were energetic and resolute. Though she was in her eighties, she had not lost her determination to simply be there for those who needed her most. At this moment, I needed her most. We wept tears of joy as we hugged each other.

She busied herself at the stove and prepared a light supper and with a pot of hot tea.

This must be a little bit what heaven is like, I thought.

"Ingrid, your house is all ready for you. Mrs. Crighton even made up your bed, and there's food in the refrigerator. Here are the keys. Let's call her and tell her that you have arrived. She will be anxious to know."

A short time later I drove down my very own driveway for the first time. I entered the door and let the sturdy, unhewn stone walls of my *Haus der Geborgenheit* put their arms around me. I was home. A house is so much more than just a space with walls around it, I thought. It's a little kingdom in itself, a place of refuge from the storms of life. The floors stand firm in spite of all the ups and downs of daily living. Here, in this safe place, I would be able to find rest on my own life's turbulent journey.

My heart sang the song of the Israelites in Psalm 126:

> *When the Lord brought back the captives who returned to Zion,*
> *We were like those who dream; (it seems so unreal).*
> *Then was our mouth filled with laughter and our tongue was singing...*
> *The Lord has done great things for us! We are glad:*
> *They who sow in tears shall reap in joy and singing...*

Outside the dining room window was a linden tree with two equally large branches emerging from the strong trunk—just like the one Walter and I had admired so often in Salzburg. The tree's presence right there, so close by my window where I could sit and admire it while eating my meals, gave me a strong sense of reassurance that I was not alone. It also reminded me to be patient with myself while letting my roots take hold in new soil.

Still, my heart ached. How I longed to share this moment with my dear husband. He had always promised that, when our youngest was college age, we would move back to the States, at least part time.

I picked up a pile of letters that had already arrived. They were addressed to:

> Ingrid Trobisch
> 2840 Natural Bridge
> Springfield, MO 65809, USA

Another strange sensation took hold of me. The address reminded me of the permanence of my decision. Had I done the right thing? I opened the letter of a dear Austrian friend who had every right to feel abandoned by me. Instead she had written the following words:

> *You are growing new roots, Ingrid. Be patient. Take the promise of Isaiah 24:6 'I will set my eyes upon (Ingrid) for good, and I will bring (her) back to this land, I will build (her) up, and not tear (her) down: I will plant (her), and not uproot (her).'*

For months, the excitement of making a new home for myself did not wear off. One of the first things I did was to rescue my father's precious library from old cardboard boxes where his books had been stored. The first furniture I purchased for the old farmhouse were bookcases. I carefully unpacked Father's books on Africa and mission history, some of them more than a hundred years old. I sensed his blessing and his presence as I leafed through them and saw his careful underlinings in red pencil.

I thought of how his children had served all over the world. My brother, John, a missionary Doctor in Tanzania, Walter and I as missionaries in Cameroun, Veda as a nurse in Tanzania, Eunie and her husband Vince in Pakistan, my brother, Carl, as a relief officer in Korea, and my other siblings at various posts in the United States.

Each week my mother, who was now 83, and I spent much time in each other's company. We came to know each other in an entirely new way. We drank tea together on what would have been her 63rd wedding anniversary and father's 94th birthday.

"Ingrid, I have missed your father every day since he left. I have been a widow for almost forty years now."

I looked at her with new admiration and understanding. She had never stopped growing as a woman, balancing her voracious appetite for reading and learning with the ever-present demands of daily life. She still managed to grow her own vegetables and gave generously from her abundance to family and friends. There was not a trace of self-pity in her. She still fed my mind and heart and was unbeatable at Scrabble.

She reminded me of the truth of the old sea captain's statement in Elizabeth Goudge's novel *The Green Dolphin*. "Three things make a man or a woman: Places where life sets us down. Folks life knocks us up against. Not the things we get, but the things we don't get."

The last was especially true in my mother's case.

Each morning in my new home I kept my promise to Mrs. Crighton, its previous owner. She had begged of me, "Stop whatever you are doing in the middle of the morning, dear Ingrid, and go sit on the porch swing with your cup of tea and listen to the birds." At the time it sounded like such a simple request. I soon discovered, though, that it is easier to get caught up in a project than to sit down and do nothing but enjoy the songs of the birds.

As I obediently rested under the shade of the old oak tree in the middle of the morning, my thoughts wandered to the many homes where I had lived, beginning with my birthplace on the slopes of Kilimanjaro. Even my first traveling home, the wicker basket that transported me from Tanzania via Europe to America in 1926, vividly entered my memories. My thoughts always led me on a journey back to Springfield and to Bethany Homestead, now just around the corner from Haus Geborgenheit. I had come back to the place where I belonged. Life had come full circle. It was okay just to sit on the porch and do nothing. I was where I was meant to be.

Early memories of my parents took up friendly residence on my new porch. I remembered those times in childhood of perfect peace when the dishes were done after our evening meal. Mother was nursing the baby before putting her down for the night. I sat with Father in the front yard facing west. The sun had gone down after a hot day, and now a heavenly breeze rose up from the southeast. We watched fireflies and falling stars from the quiet perch of our folding camp chairs. And my father told me about Africa—about sitting just like this after a long day's safari.

Later in Africa, Walter and I were enchanted by the same magical hour between twilight and darkness in front of our thatch-roofed mud hut in Tchollire. We would sit and sit, studying the vast expanse of sky, listening to the sounds of the African night, traveling many miles in spirit to our distant loved ones, and moving closer to each other after long hours of tiring daylight labor.

Oddly enough, these times of purposeful dreaming led to a burst of new energy in my life. My theme verse became II Chronicles 28:20, "Be strong and courageous, and do the work. Do not be afraid or discouraged, for the Lord God, my God is with you. He will not fail you or forsake you until all the work for the service of the temple of the Lord is finished."

My first project was to translate Walter's last book manuscript, *The Misunderstood Man*, into English and complete the last chapter that he had left only in outline form. Each day I listened to my Shepherd's voice and tried to follow His instructions as I filled out the bare branches of the manuscript tree. I felt as if Walter had dictated this chapter to me personally.

Later a reviewer remarked about this book, published after Walter's death, "One can see that this book is published posthumously, for the first two chapters have been tampered with. But the last chapter is genuine Walter Trobisch." My son David, who had helped with the editing and final German edition, and I looked at each other. It was just this last chapter that we had spent so much time working on together. David at the time was teaching New Testament at the University of Heidelberg. We both felt this book was one of Walter's best. *The Pain of Being a Man* Walter had humorously dubbed it, in contrast to my book, *The Joy of Being a Woman*. In his prologue Walter wrote:

> *We must play the role of the strong sex, and therefore, we need someone to understand us in our weakness. Or as the African driver had painted on his small bus in Accra, Ghana, 'Man is suffering, but woman don't know it.'*

The last words Walter wrote on this earth were for the epilogue of this book. I wept as I read them:

> *Part of being redeemed means being satisfied with what is temporary and provisional and imperfect on this earth. Even if you never reach your goal, it is good to be going in the right direction.*
>
> *I was born during the next to last hour of the next to last day of the next to last month of the year. This has been a paradigm for my life, a challenge to courageously accept what is incomplete. Yet as the foundation on which we stand, from which we originate and out of which we live, we have only the ultimate completeness, the final reality.*
>
> *Christ is the final reality. Everything else exists only as shadow. His love penetrates and radiates through us and gives us life.*

Besides completing the satisfying writing projects on my desk, I helped organize and conduct our first Family Life Retreats in the United States. My son Daniel came from Austria to help me and to train the first leader-couples. We called them Quiet Waters Retreats. Singles as well as couples were included. This ongoing ministry takes place in many different parts of the United States.

Our goal is simple: to release *couple power*. In order to do this, *single power* has first to be set free. This means learning to become a whole person. "God is constantly calling us to be more than we are," Madeleine l'Engle puts it, "and to break down our defenses of self-protection in order to be free to receive and give love."

And what is *couple power*? It's the multiplied power of two whole people joined as man and wife. Two people together can do more than two separately, especially when they know that as man and woman they have been created in the image of God. Together they mirror His image to the world.

Soren Kierkegaard once said, "Each one of us needs an idea for which he is ready to live and to die." In other words, we need to find our passion and allow ourselves the satisfaction of a cause worth fighting for.

"What is my passion?" I found it needful to ask myself. I could only answer, "To release couple power!" I knew in the depths of my soul that, for both men and women, a committed marriage to one's best friend is a wonderful source of well-being and a firm foundation for healthy family life. Instead of watching couples bail water out of a sinking marriage boat, I felt a strong need to help men and women find new ways to repair the leaks that were causing them to sink.

In 1980, while still in Europe, I was elected to the board of the International Federation for Family Life Promotion as member-at-large. IFFLP was a non-governmental organization with Dr. Claude Lanctot as executive director with offices in Washington, D.C. Five medical doctors served as regional directors for Europe, Asia-Oceania, Africa, South and North America. As a board we met annually often in connection with training seminars for family life leaders throughout the world. An emphasis was placed on fertility awareness and the latest scientific discoveries in the field of natural family planning. The six years I spent on the IFFLP Board were for me rich, mind-stretching tears as I traveled to Columbia, Chile, Kenya, Madagascar, Mauritius, Hong Kong, Ireland, Canada, and Poland. My daughter Ruth, at the time a medical student in Vienna, was my companion on the African tour. Nothing will take away those joyful memories and mutual friendships with world and local leaders who believe that the future of the family is the future of the world.

Now that I had come home to my *safe place*, I was ready in a new and passionate way to give myself to this calling. The walls of *Haus Geborgenheit* and beyond them the strong arms of my Heavenly Father would shelter me from any storm. My life vessel had found anchor in a lovely harbor.

Ruth, Stephen, Ingrid, David
Daniel and Katrine

ELEVEN

LONGING (SEHNSUCHT)

"The journey is the reward."
~Anonymous~

We all need someone who waits for us, someone who lets us know when we are missed, someone who thinks and dreams with us. In the months after my dramatic move across continents, *Haus Geborgenheit* quickly became a place of hospitality. My life filled itself up in many ways. I learned anew the joy of providing shelter and sharing meals with those I loved, with family and friends from all over the world. On the other hand I could not deny my longing for a strong partner. One sultry summer day I wrote in my journal:

> *'Let not your longing slay the appetite for living,' Jim Elliott told his fiancée Elisabeth when they were separated by continents. After a Family Life Retreat at Schloss Mansfeld in East Germany in May 1991 with 23 couples, another one in June, teaching and interacting with 23 couples at Mount Carmel, Minnesota and again a week of teaching in July at the InterVarsity Family Camp at Cedar Campus, Michigan-again with 23 couples—I'm aching inside with longing. I give it to you, Lord—You who are my Steadfast Love.*

Back home at *Haus Geborgenheit*, I recovered from this strenuous schedule. Long and lonely walks through the rolling hills of my neighborhood rendered my heart even more restless.

What joy it would be to simply hold a loving hand and quietly drink in the beauty of the evening together. I asked the Lord why there was no one I could talk to, with whom I could look in the same direction—explore the same views—listen to the same music.

Again it was Walter who came to my rescue. I found what he had written specifically for singles many years earlier. It was as if he were coaching me through these long days of intense longing and solitude:

> *Love is a feeling to be learned by the single person. Those who do not marry do not have to give up love, but they have to learn love that gives up —just as those who are married must learn it. One could even say that the desire to be married is the condition for a happy single life.*
>
> *Though the task we have to face is the same, whether we are married or single, let us not make the mistake of thinking that our present state is permanent. Let us not burden our hearts with the fear of finality.*
>
> *Marriage can be a task for a limited time and then it suddenly ends with the death of one partner. Being single can also be but a passing task. God does not like the decision for a lifetime that we make out of resignation and disappointment. He wants us to live our life this day and to discover all the joyous possibilities of it with confidence and courage.*

I also heard what my niece, Ann, said after a distressing divorce. She had achieved the professional goals she had set for herself, but still she admitted to me:

> *I do miss one thing, I miss being married. I am not desperate for a husband. I believe I could live the rest of my life well without one. My son is a source of joy, and our times together are filled with tenderness and meaningful communicating. But there is a void in my life. I want to share it with another flesh and blood, made-in-the-image-of-God human being.*
>
> *My parents' lives have shown me the deep happiness and fulfillment that comes from having a committed and loving mate. Were the right person to come along, I would be ready to go. I would not be afraid of*

leaving a well thought-out 'career track' because my main career track is one that leads home. Home to Him that is the Author and Perfecter of our lives.

My heart echoed Ann's words. I shared with her what my pastor of fifty years, William Berg, had asked me, "Ingrid, why did you never marry again after Walter's death?"

"Because," I told him, "I have never met a man all these years whom I could love more than my children."

"What a foolish answer!" Ann said. "Don't you know that you love a husband in a different way than you love a child?" She was right.

Over the years I have observed that it is hard for any man on this earth to come into those deep recesses of a woman's heart and fill all her needs. Only one, Jesus Christ, can do that. And yet it is perhaps a woman's greatest anxiety—to be unloved. If I could tell my three sons only one thing about what it means to be good husbands, it would be this: "Every day, give your wife the assurance of your love—tell her she is number one in your life." And she must learn to hear and accept what he is telling her, both by his words and his deeds.

A woman can only do this if she has a sense of selfworth, honest self-acceptance. Otherwise the affirming and up-building words of the one who loves her will go through her heart like a sieve. Every Sunday in our liturgy, we confess the sin of not loving God with our whole heart, of not loving our neighbor as ourselves, and of not loving ourselves as we should. How hard it is for me to do just that and accept honest compliments with grace.

Before my marriage to Walter, I had been single for 26 years. Now, after his death, I had again been single for twenty years. It is strange how we always long for what we do not have. My eldest son, Daniel, a psychotherapist in Salzburg, often says when counseling, "There's only one thing harder than living alone—and that is living with another person. But only if you have first learned to live alone are you ready to live success-fully with another person."

What about remarriage? Could I ever love again? My inner dialogue with Walter continued. Through his books it was as if he pulled his chair next to mine whenever I needed reassurance. He wrote in *Love Is a Feeling to Be Learned*:

> *Love is tension and fulfillment.*
> *It is deep longing and hostility.*
> *It is gladness and it is pain.*
> *There is not one without the other.*
> *Happiness is only a part of love—this is what has to be learned.*
> *Suffering belongs to love also.*
> *This is the mystery of love, its beauty and its burden.*
> *Love is a feeling to be learned.*
> *The art of giving up, of renouncing, is also the secret of happiness in a single person's life. To give up one's self is as important for a single person as it is for one who is married.*
> *Those who learn this art will never be lonesome, even if they are single. Those who don't will always be lonesome, even though they are married. The task we have to face is the same, whether we are married or single: To live a fulfilled life in spite of many unfulfilled desires.*[4]

In his own way, Walter challenged me to face this task over and over again. I continued to look for deeper secrets of the happy, single life. I learned that it is possible to live a full and complete life without the expression of physical sexuality, but that it is not possible to live without love and affirmation and meaningful relationships. We have to face our loneliness and know that our destiny is not controlled by our sexual desires, but by our minds.

My favorite aunt, who had spent most of her life as a single woman, told me, "Ingrid, a woman is always in love with someone, but infatuation doesn't take the real person into account. Love can start only when you see the real person, not the one you've made up."

The decision to live a chaste life is a decision to be free. It gives us inner strength and a spiritual energy that helps break the bonds of selfishness.

I learned a new perspective during my years as a single woman. I did not look at what I had given up, but instead I looked at my precious gift of freedom. I could enjoy people of all ages and take pleasure in beauty—whether it was a sunset, a concert or a work of art. And I whole-heartedly agreed with Kathleen Norris that, "The fruit of celibacy is hospitality." One of my greatest joys was to learn, first of all, to be a good hostess to myself, and then to others.

My family continues to grow. My five children all have found loving partners. As I page through my journal I read:

Today is my youngest daughter's 30th birthday. She was born right after an African cloudburst in our little mission hospital. Before she was even an hour old, I got up off the delivery table, climbed into our Willys Jeep and was driven to the straw-roofed guesthouse where all of the family—father, big sister Katrine and three brothers— gathered around my bed and we celebrated. What a beginning!

Five days later she was baptized at the Sunday morning service in the African chapel at Garoua-Boulai.

Now she is a wife, a doctor, mother of Raffael and Paul, and living in Vienna with her gifted musician husband, Ernst. She's a wise, generous, and beautiful young woman. As I write this I listen to the sound track of Out of Africa and wonder where her next decade will lead her.

Lord, she is your child. Help her to be a child of Light in all she does and to follow the Lamb.

My life's circles keep widening. The little tree of Family Life Mission which Walter and I had planted keeps growing. FLM, as we call it, has its roots in the Word of God and sound psychological principles. We are convinced that the family is the best landing place for the Gospel in today's world. The one who says, "I am the Way, the Truth and the Life," is the only one who can bring true life to parched marriages, and fulfillment to those who are not married. Now FLM has an active ministry in Africa, in Europe, and in the United States.

At the end of each Quiet Waters Retreat the participants are asked to write a love letter to their spouse. Those who are not married write a love letter to Jesus. This is what I wrote after one of our seminars:

> *Dear lover of my soul,*
>
> *There's no one to write my love letter to on this earth. My heart longs to express love—all the love that Walter through his faithful love awoke in my heart and which since his death I have tried to channel to others.*
>
> *I have no hope—and hope deferred makes the heart heavy—that I will ever have an earthly partner and so I give you my crushed heart, Lord, knowing that squeezed grapes can make good wine.*
>
> *There are tears as I go down this lonely road. I would so much love to have a firm shoulder on which to rest my head. I do as John the beloved disciple did, and rest my head on your shoulder, Jesus.*
>
> *'O give thanks to the Lord, for He is good, for his steadfast love endures forever.' Psalm 106:1*
>
> *Dear Jesus, I take you as my heavenly bridegroom.*
>
> *Love, Ingrid Johanna*

One day in 1997 I found a letter in my mailbox from a Lutheran pastor asking me to send my book *Hidden Strength* to his seven adult children. I knew his name because his older brother had been a spiritual mentor for us in college. As students, his sister and I had been roommates. Doris had told me of her younger brother Lauren who was serving in the army medical corps in World War II. I had briefly met him at his brother's wedding in 1946.

A few weeks after Lauren's letter arrived, I received the sad news from a mutual friend that Lauren's wife had died after a short bout with cancer. My friend asked me to send a copy of my book *Learning to Walk Alone* as her gift to Lauren. Several months later he came to Springfield to visit my sister

Eunie and her husband Vince, one of his boyhood friends. My sister invited me to their church and to dinner afterwards. Katrine, my oldest daughter, was visiting at the time and joined us.

"What a fine man!" she said to me after the service. "When he sang 'My Jesus, I Love Thee' and talked about the sudden death of his wife, I knew that he was honestly working through his grief and that he was not just putting a quick Band-Aid on his wound." Lauren impressed me too. I liked him and felt comfortable in his presence.

In a few weeks I would be speaking at a Grief Seminar in Minnesota, his home state, so I invited him to attend. He did, and we had some deep talks about our own experiences of loss. He was a year older than I, had served as a parish pastor for 26 years, and then had gone into the chaplaincy. Two months after he had retired, just when they were hoping to travel together, Norma, his beloved wife of 47 years died.

A few months later we saw each other again at our college reunion. We discovered that Lauren had known Walter before I had. Walter had spent a year at Augustana Seminary as the first German graduate student. They had been in the same Bible study group.

It felt as if deep roots had intertwined below the surface of our lives over many years without us even knowing it. We had inherited the same legacy from our Swedish grandparents which one theologian respectfully dubbed "uncomplicated Swedish Lutheran piety." We had attended the same schools and had been taught the same values. As young adults we had both committed ourselves to a life of service, and God had blessed us beyond measure. Now we had become good friends, but nothing more.

I wrote in my journal how easy and uncomplicated it was to be with Lauren at our Luther College reunion:

Today I felt so safe in a booth at Wigwam Cafe with him beside me. 'Ingrid, you like to be sheltered, don't you?' Lauren said. At the morning church service he sat in the pew in front of me. I was

very conscious of his presence. I wondered if he was aware of mine.
'Is he your brother?' a woman asked me. 'He has a wonderful voice.'
'Yes, he's my brother,' I said. 'He is also my friend.'

In July 1999 I attended the International Renovaré Conference in Houston where Richard Foster and Dallas Willard were speaking. Two thousand people had gathered. At the closing session, each one was invited to come forward to receive a blessing. A warm, glowing African-American woman put her hands on my head.

"Go back home and have fun," she said. "You have worked hard, and God has seen it. Your latter days will be even more fruitful than your former days. Continue to bear fruit and don't be *paralyzed by grace*, as Richard Foster puts it. Let Jesus live his life in and through you."

Back at home later that year a spectacular fall made my heart rejoice. The leaves were ablaze with color and the air was cool and bracing. I took my morning walk and picked up the daily mail. As I leafed through the letters, I saw that there was one from Lauren. I forced myself to slowly walk back to the house and to sit in my favorite letter-reading chair before I cautiously opened it. With wide eyes of wonder I took in how his words and feelings had spilled onto the page. God had been speaking to him about leaving the past behind, he wrote, and about looking ahead…

> *Ingrid, the emotions I kept well hidden underneath that I dared not show, broke loose and the floodgates opened; I saw new light and I began to understand where I was really at. I saw that my relationship to you was far more than friendship, that I loved you. Then the pent-up emotions that I didn't want to listen to or acknowledge opened up to me a new world… A new emotion of love and caring has gripped me. I do not apologize for this.*

Thus began the whirlwind romance between Lauren and myself. On many days I felt downright giddy, just like a teenager. Our friendship quickly advanced to a new level of sharing and adventure. The phone bills also quickly advanced to new heights! My heart danced and danced with awed disbelief.

A precious friend walked in my door one morning and said, "I wish I were single because then I could do what I want to do."

That prompted me to ask myself, "Was there anything I did not do because I was married to Walter?" We had always talked matters over, and then we made them possible. We were a team to help each other find joy, and we tried not to stand in each other's way. Only after Walter died, did I truly recognize his stature.

In my journal I tried to find words for Lauren's stature:

1. He is a beautiful man—tall, kind face, good hands.
2. He loves the Lord.
3. A man of prayer: "I pray for you every day."
4. A lover of music and a singer.
5. A compassionate friend to his friends.
6. A pastor who loves to share the Word.
7. A family man—faithful father to his three sons and four daughters.
8. Loves to travel.
9. Comfortable to be with.
10. I'd be proud to introduce him to my friends and family.

Then I remembered my childhood prayers for my future husband. I had always pictured him as a tall Swede!

I went to Communion in my home church early one Sunday morning. As I knelt at the altar and prayed, I saw Walter as I often did, but this time in a long white pastor's robe. He was not looking at me, but at Lauren dressed in a similar robe. Walter said to him, "Lauren, I covered her all these years. Now it's your turn."

After attending a Quiet Waters Retreat in Springfield, Lauren proposed to me, and I said yes to him.

We asked Pastor Berg to be our wedding pastor. He had known us both since our student days and was now 90 years old. He gave us his joyous blessing "to be good companions for the rest of the journey."

Our joy of anticipation was great. Again phone bills soared sky-high as we notified children and relatives and friends around the world. We both had to face serious questioning from loving and protective family members. This was a new and quite humorous situation for two mature adults in their seventies!

Women of my own generation seemed to respond in one of two ways. Some said they could never take such a leap of faith again that late in life. Others told me in unison, "Go for it!"

My own daughters were bemused by the sudden role reversal. When Katrine tried to help me with my lipstick before the wedding ceremony, I giggled and told her that Lauren liked to kiss it off. At first she thought that I was kidding. Well, I wasn't!

On the wedding day, November 27, 1999, our twelve children met each other for the first time. This was God's wonderful answer to our most fervent prayer. Our six daughters and six sons stood right beside us during the festive ceremony at St. Mark's Cathedral in Minneapolis. As we knelt at the altar, they all placed their hands on our heads and blessed us.

The rest of the journey could now begin.

Lauren and Ingrid at home

TWELVE

FULL CIRCLE

"We are not truly at home anywhere until
we reach the Father's house."
~Eugene Peterson~

It is difficult to write this chapter because I am still very
much living it, trying to squeeze out every ounce of new joy
from my shared life with Lauren. He and I are seated together
under the shade of our ancient oak tree. We are by now in
our third year of marriage and have gently settled into our
new home across the road from Haus Geborgenheit.

For twenty years I walked alone. I watched joyfully as my
children found their life partners. I was deeply grateful that
they too believed in having children. I have ten handsome
grandsons and four strong granddaughters. When Walter and
I were asked how parents could make their children become
believers, our answer was always, "You can't. It can only
happen by the grace of God. You have to give birth to a child
over and over again. The umbilical cord has to be cut repeatedly in order to give your child complete freedom, and you
have to risk everything on God."

While it is good to talk to your children about God, it is
just as important to talk to God about your children. Faith
does not happen by using forceful means, nor does it happen
through good advice or well-intended protection. Faith

comes as a gift and is helped by God's Holy Spirit whose presence cannot be forced on anyone.

I just sent my 18-year-old grandson Charles an e-mail. Yes, we grandmothers have also joined the age of electronic communication! Charles had told me on the phone about his serious, but unsuccessful search for God. My message to him was simple, "Instead of trying to find God, let yourself be found by Him. When I caught on to that truth it revolutionized my life."

Looking back, I see there have been many days of unbelievable joy for me when I literally felt like I was walking on water. One such day was in 1975 when my daughter, Katrine, still a student, called me from Wellesley College, telling me that she had made a decision for Christ. Beautiful light streamed into Walter's and my dark world that day. In a little shop in Salzburg I bought an expensive silk scarf to send her. Its colors were like a blaze of autumn light to signify her new beginning.

A more recent day of overflowing joy was my wedding day when Lauren and I were blessed by those whom we love most in this world. We both knew that Walter and Lauren's wife, Norma, joined us in spirit for that historic blessing and that they were themselves celebrating with us.

Many times my thoughts take me to my wonderful mother and her complete devotion to my father and her children. When I was a senior in college, I asked her if it had not been a great sacrifice for her to become the mother of ten children. We were riding together in the old Packard on our way from Wahoo in Nebraska to Springfield in Missouri with the remnant of all her household goods packed into it. She had been a widow then for five years and was preparing to go to Bolivia to be the housemother at an orphanage.

She stepped on the brakes and turned to me. "Sacrifice! I considered it the highest honor God could give to a woman, to be the mother of the children of Ralph Hult."

She was my father's ear, always ready to listen to his ideas and plans and to follow his dreams. With cheerful optimism she had warmed and fed us, and at the same time had educated us, for she had trained to be an English teacher. In her children she never tolerated poor grammar or pronunciation. I don't recall her demanding anything for herself. At the age of ninety, she simply said, "As you grow older, you learn to live with less."

You can only measure the length of a tree when it is cut down. This truth gripped my heart when Mother died at the age of 92, her five sons and five daughters mourning her passing.

I thought of my other experiences of death, the terrible pain I tried to cover up when Father died. Mother told us that he was a hero, and he would not want us to grieve. But I could never again feel his warm arms around me or hear his word of approval—those words a young daughter needs so desperately to hear if she is to know who she is.

I thought of my beloved grandmother, how she had called me to her bedside when she was dying and gave me her blessing to follow my call to Africa. My little sister was with me as grandmother breathed her last. Mary said, "I don't know whether to cry because she is dead or laugh because she is with Jesus."

And then I thought of Mutti, my dear mother-in-law who died in our little home on the Lichtenberg just twelve years before her son. She died in the midst of winter—he, on the most beautiful day of the harvest.

Again my thoughts traveled to Walter and the incredible impact he had on my life's journey. During our engagement, Walter and I wrote down the qualities we were looking for in our life partner. This is what I wrote on January 3, 1952, six months before our marriage:

My husband must be one for whom love and obedience to God comes first even before personal wishes and desires to please his partner. This love for God is best described, Walter, in your own words:

'Life with a pulsing heart. Glow and storm and swing. Life out of a strength that knows no end—like being caught in the strong current of a river. Being carried to a goal for which the heart is longing. A life straight towards God—not always looking to the right or the left. Not mourning over what is left behind. Doing quickly and without procrastination the work at hand.

'Leaving behind that which is beyond my ability. But glowing brightly for the present moment and taking complete advantage of its opportunities. This love to God is a youthful feeling of life. It has the ease of godly carelessness and the glow of full surrender. Love to God is life out of an eternal satisfaction. The secret of this life is obedience.'

Walter had walked before me with his vibrant and pulsating faith, in life and in death.

When a tree is harvested, the rings in its trunk reveal its age—how it has grown from the heart outward over the years. As I look back, I can see these ever-widening circles, like rings of a felled tree. Each ring has brought me in contact with new people and life-changing experiences. I am thankful and sing in my heart that old Swedish hymn:

All the way my Savior leads me. What have I to ask beside?
Can I doubt his tender mercy who through life has been my guide?

My favorite time of day is late afternoon. Now I deeply identify with that time in my life. I like to think of Lauren and myself as basking in the glorious light of our sunset years. We need the evening light upon life in order to understand it. The blaze of day is often blinding. Philip Howard says, "When shadows fall and light flows eastward along our own levels, we see much that we never could see until then. When it is evening the light is mellow." Life needs the mellow light for its interpretation.

I am traveling between two eternities—from birth to death. It has been my privilege to see many pages in the book that is this world, as St. Augustine puts it. My life has been one of ever-widening circles. Happiness is making the best possible use of these experiences and giving them meaning as I continue my journey homeward.

A friend wrote in her Christmas letter:

When He decides it's harvest time for any of us, His long-held grasp on the heart of our tree will lift the circles of our life farther up and farther in. If we could just see clearly, I think our wooden rings would turn gold as they spiral on up into His light and are transformed in the circle of His love.

Sometimes leaving home is more what you leave behind than knowing what is ahead. When my oldest daughter was 19, she left our home on the Lichtenberg and traveled on the last westward voyage of the *SS France* from Europe to the United States. As they sailed into the sunset, she spent most of her time on deck—not on the forward deck, but in the rear, looking at the wake, transfixed by it, and thinking of the world she was choosing to leave behind. She knew that she needed to leave home in order to find a new beginning in her life.

On a recent trip back to Austria, I walked up the steep path to the summit of our Lichtenberg Mountain, the place where we had lived for 18 years. A humid, warm breeze called a Foehn—dangerous to people with heart trouble—touched my cheeks. Maybe it was this breeze that caused Walter's heart to fail that October morning more than two decades ago.

I've traveled on a long road since then. It's been an uphill climb all the way, except when our thoughtful Lord gave me a bench to rest on. I try hard during these evening years to keep a steady rhythm between working and resting. So many thoughts circle my heart like random, beautiful butterflies. After a daily power nap, I derive much joy from sharing with Lauren what is in my heart, whether it is serious or silly. He always listens. Sometimes we're just quiet while we hold hands and sip our afternoon coffee. We don't know how many more days we have left to sit and watch the setting sun, so with open hands we simply receive every hour together as a marvelous gift.

I have been deeply influenced by all whom I have met and walked alongside on this journey home. My father was a solemn man whom I loved with all my heart. I used to make him little surprise gifts to put under his plate so that his face would light up—even if just for a moment. I loved to walk with him. I had to take two steps to his one, so then I thought if I skipped I could even fly a little. And I did.

My youngest sister, Mary, was only seven when our father died in Dar-es-Salaam and was buried there in a lonely grave on the very same day. Her son, Jim, wrote from his mission trip to Finland:

> *I watched a man dancing with his tiny daughter—spinning, smiling, laughing. It was so beautiful, I almost cried. What a perfect picture of God the Father. He says to us, 'Come and dance with me, child. Let's spin and smile our eternity together! Let's enjoy life!'*
>
> *What a fun thought that some day your Daddy Ralph will greet you in heaven and say, 'Come dance with me, Mary. I've been waiting to see you for so long. Do you know how much I love you, baby girl?' Then he will take you by the hand and embrace you with a hug like you've never had before—full of the love of the many long years of waiting to be with you. He will guide you into the most joyful dance of your life!*

Some day we won't have to dance alone here on earth, but will have all eternity to be with our loved ones. A joyful awareness of another reality is slowly seeping into my life. We are but sojourners here. Another home is waiting that means the end of all waiting.

Katrine and Ingrid at a book signing

AN AFTERWORD

Katrine Stewart

For me it is no use to write unless the words spill forth from the heart.

Twenty years after my father, Walter Trobisch, died I was to stand at my mother's side as she pledged her love to Lauren Youngdale on November 27, 1999 in St. Mark's Cathedral in Minneapolis, Minnesota. Mother was 73 years old. Nothing has been quite the same since then.

Up until her wedding day she had been feverishly working on her autobiography. I offered to take the manuscript off her desk and simply watch what would unfold.

The text draws freely from Mother's initial draft. I have woven her words into animated vignettes strewn like highlights throughout her incredible life. The chronological sequence of events takes second place to their significance in Mother's life and the lives of those closely linked to hers.

We laughed and cried as we sat in front of the computer screen together and journeyed through Mother's life. Some painful memories found healing while others turned into pure joy as we searched for the right words. I thank my God for a mother who shows me the way home, leading from fear and darkness into His glorious light.

Katrine Trobisch Stewart
March 2002

Footnotes:

[1] Ernst Jaeschke, *Bruno Gutman, His Life, His Thoughts, and His Work: An Early Attempt At a Theology In an African Context* (Erlangen: Verlag der Ev.-Luth. Mission, 1985).

[2] Ingrid Trobisch, *Bright Legacy* (Ann Arbor, MI: Servant Publications, 1985).

[3] For a humorous account of Walter's trip with four children across continents see David Trobisch, *The Adventures of Pumpelhoober* (Bolivar: Quiet Waters Publications, 2000).

[4] Walter Trobisch, *Love Yourself & Love Is a Feeling to be Learned* (Bolivar: Quiet Waters Publications, 2001).

Quiet Waters Publications
P.O. Box 34, Bolivar MO 65613-0034
http://www.quietwaterspub.com
Email: QWP@usa.net

On Our Way Rejoicing

By Ingrid Trobisch

Ingrid Trobisch, tells the story of what happens when God takes away the father of ten children. A whole family is called to service and sent into the world. The story surges with movement, partings and reunion, sorrows and joys, adventure and romance, shining courage, and above all, the warm love that knits together a large Christian family.

ISBN 0-9663966-2-6

Keeper of the Springs

By Ingrid Trobisch, Marlee Alex, Katrine Stewart

This artfully illustrated coffee table book provides inspiration and motivation for cultivating atmosphere, tradition, and beauty in ordinary and hectic surroundings

Love Yourself & Love is a Feeling to Be Learned

By Walter Trobisch

Love your neighbor as you love yourself and not instead of yourself. Happiness is only a part of love. Suffering belongs to love also. This is the mystery of love, its beauty and its burden. Love is a feeling to be learned.

ISBN 1-931475-06-7

I Loved A Girl

By Walter Trobisch

'Last Friday, I loved a girl—or as you would put it, I committed adultery.' This deeply moving story of a young African couple is Walter Trobisch's first book. It has become a classic with its frank answers to frank questions about sex and love. Its tremendous worldwide success led Walter and Ingrid Trobisch to leave their missionary post in Cameroun and start an international ministry as marriage and family counselors.

ISBN 1-931475-01-6

I Married You

By Walter Trobisch

Set in a large African city, this story covers only four days in the life of Walter and Ingrid Trobisch. Nothing in this book is fiction. All the stories have really happened. The people involved are still living today. The direct, sensitive, and compassionate narrative presents Christian marriage as a dynamic triangle.

ISBN 0-9663966-6-9

The Adventures Of Pumpelhoober

By David Trobisch, illustrated by Eva Bruchmann

"In Austria they call someone who has a lot of bad luck, 'Pumpelhoober.' I, too, often have bad luck," Walter and Ingrid Trobisch's nine year old son David explains his nickname. This humorous children's book tells the story of the Trobisch family in Africa from the perspective of a child.

ISBN 0-9663966-4-2

A Book of Life: Spiritual Journaling in the Twenty-First Century

By Katrine Trobisch Stewart

Katrine Stewart's insights into the art of journal keeping entertain as well as challenge us to sit down and begin our very own "book of life" in word and image. The author describes fun and practical ways in which to capture our fragmented modern lives and also emphasizes the role of the journal as a time-tested tool for spiritual discernment.

ISBN 0-9663966-8-5